EDUCATION IN DEVELOPING AREAS

EDUCATION IN
DEVELOPING AREAS

DON ADAMS
Director, Center for Development Education
Syracuse University

and

ROBERT M. BJORK
Chairman, Department of Economics and Sociology
George Peabody College for Teachers

DAVID McKAY COMPANY, INC.
NEW YORK

EDUCATION IN DEVELOPING AREAS

LIBRARY OF CONGRESS CATALOG CARD NUMBER: 68-31208

MANUFACTURED IN THE UNITED STATES OF AMERICA

Dedication

To the students at the Center for Development Education.

Introduction

The challenge and the complexities of the task of fulfilling the minimum aspirations of the peoples in the underdeveloped regions of the world are unsurpassed by any human endeavor except possibly the search for lasting peace. In the most fundamental sense, development is an educational process whereby people learn to understand and alter constructively their relations to their natural and social environments. Learning how to produce more food, provide new modes of employment, and create new values to guide men's lives demands a high degree of intranational and international cooperative effort. Being as complicated as life itself, many aspects of the development process remain very much a mystery. A few decades of intensive experience have clearly demonstrated that the facts of poverty are not going to be erased by eloquent statements of world or national leaders, by the messianic spirit of local cultists, or by the small dosages of antipoverty vaccine currently being offered by the developed nations.

Next perhaps to the emphasis placed on economic growth as the key process in development has been the attention given to education. Many leaders and intellectuals in the developing countries of the world have high expectations concerning formal education as an important lever in uplifting and transforming their societies. Perhaps their hopes in this regard are too high, but that they intend rapidly to push educational development is evident.

This book is meant to survey some aspects of the role of education in the progress of society. It attempts to point out the general contrasts between developed and underdeveloped societies and some of the actions and obstacles involved in the making of developed social orders (Chapter I). The particular focus of the discussion throughout is the possible role and problems of formal education in the development of nations. An effort is made to identify the contribution education has made in the formation and maintenance of developed societies with a view toward bringing the present problems of the poor nations into some perspective (Chapter II). Three regions of the world faced with generally underdeveloped conditions have been chosen for special attention: Middle Africa, South Asia, and Latin America. The educational poverty of these regions is discussed in some detail with the emphasis put on both the similarities and the dissimilarities the different regions face in improving the spread and quality of their schools and in utilizing education as a force for development (Chapters III, IV, and V). Some of the major and persistent educational problems of these regions (and the poor nations in general) are singled out for special discussion in Chapter VI.

The related issues of improving education in quantity and quality and the linking of education to national development aspirations are the recurring themes throughout the book. Chapter VII discusses the manner and potential of making national education decisions planfully in the cause of development. Educational projections, targets, and financial allocations are receiving more rational attention today than ever before, and the reader should have at least a general idea of the kinds of issues involved in these planning endeavors.

This book does not purport to penetrate deeply into very specific educational trends in particular nations or into the more sophisticated efforts to theorize about or quantify the relation of education to economic, political, or other aspects of development. Rather, the effort here is to give the nonspecialized student an overview of a question that has captured more and more interest over the past two decades, namely, the place of education in improving the life of the masses of people in the vast stretches of the world now labeled underdeveloped.

Table of Contents

INTRODUCTION.. vii

LIST OF TABLES xii

Chapter

I   DEFINING DEVELOPMENT........................ 1
    Historical Views of Development 1
    Current Development Terminology and
      Description 4
    Modern Theories of Development 7
      Rostow versus the Marxian View................. 7
      Empirical Educational Development 9
      Social Differentiation................................ 10
      Vicious Circle and Beneficent Circle Theories
        of Development 12
    Summary... 15
    Suggested Readings 19

II   THE CONTRIBUTION OF EDUCATION
    TO DEVELOPMENT................................... 20
    Education in the Already Developed Societies 20
      England 23
      Japan 31
    Education in the Development of Today's Less
      Developed Societies.............................. 36
    Population and Education 38
    Education and the Economy 42
    Education and the Polity 43
    Summary... 45
    Suggested Readings 46

III   PATTERNS OF EDUCATIONAL
    POVERTY: MIDDLE AFRICA..................... 47
    Colonial Educational Policies........................ 49
      British Policy 49
      French Policy.. 50
      Belgian Policy 52

Intraregional Forces for Continuity and Change
    in Education 53
The Effect of Colonization by Europeans 54
The Effects of Language Diversity 55
The Effects of Rural Predominance and
    Recent Urbanization........................... 56
Cultural Variations in Receptivity to Change ... 58
Education and the Achievement of National
    Goals... 60
Diffusion of Education through Classes and
    Regions 61
Education and the Modernization of African
    Values... 65
Educational Planning 67
New Directions...................................... 71
Summary.. 73
Suggested Readings 74

IV   PATTERNS OF EDUCATIONAL
    POVERTY: SOUTH ASIA 76
Colonial Educational Policies........................ 76
The Social Context of Educational Development.. 79
    Language Diversity.................................. 79
    Religious and Value Systems...................... 80
Education and Social Change........................ 83
    Village and Urban Problems 83
    Population Change and Education................ 86
    Educational Planning and Priorities 88
Resistance to the Changing Character of
    Schooling.. 94
Summary.. 97
Suggested Readings 98

V   PATTERNS OF EDUCATIONAL
    POVERTY: LATIN AMERICA...................... 100
Colonial Educational Policies........................ 100
Obstacles to Educational Development 102
    The "Indian" Problem 102
    Population Change 103

Inhibitive Value Structure 103
Development Goals and Educational Change 105
Educational Planning 105
Population Change and Education 107
Rural Development and Education 109
Dissemination of Education 110
Problems of Secondary Education 113
Problems at the University Level 116
Summary 120
Suggested Readings 121

VI   SOME COMMON EDUCATIONAL PROBLEMS
     IN THE DEVELOPING NATIONS 123
Shortage of Qualified Teachers 124
Failure of Schools to Hold Students 125
Inappropriate Nature of Curricula 127
The Imbalance between Rural and Urban
     Advancement 129
Problem of Female Participation in Educational
     Development 131
The Monopolization of Higher Graduates by
     Government and the Higher Professions 133
Lingering Conservatism in the Values Found in
     Educational Systems 134
Summary 137
Suggested Readings 139

VII EDUCATIONAL PLANNING FOR
     NATIONAL DEVELOPMENT 140
Defining Educational Planning 141
Determining Goals and Targets 143
Criticism of the Social and Manpower
     Approaches 148
Obstacles to Precision in Assessing Educational
     Needs 151
Some Operational Problems 154
Summary 156
Suggested Readings 158

INDEX 159

List of Tables

Table

III–1. Distribution of Working Population and Money Income in Nyasaland (Malawi), 1954 and 1960 61

III–2. Comparison of Federal and African Systems of Education in Northern Rhodesia (Zambia), *circa* 1962 ... 63

III–3. School Enrollment Targets for Africa.................... 69

III–4. African Higher Educational Enrollment Targets...... 70

III–5. Percentage of Senior Public Service Positions Filled by Africans, Various Countries, 1960 70

IV–1. Percentage of Literates among Different Castes and Communities, India, *circa* 1960 84

IV–2. Desire for Family Limitation among 1,525 Urban Indian Women, Various Educational Levels, *circa* 1960 87

IV–3. South Asian Educational and Occupational Data, *circa* 1960.. 89

IV–4. Primary Enrollments (in Millions) in 1960 and Target Figures for 1970 and 1980, Three South Asian Nations 92

IV–5. Percentage of Allocations of First Pakistani Five-Year Plan to Various Aspects of Education, East and West Pakistan, Implemented, 1955–1960 96

V–1. Primary and Secondary Enrollment as Percentage of Appropriate Age Groups (5–14 and 15–19) in Thirteen Latin American Countries 106

V–2. Percentage of Appropriate Age Group in Each of the First Eight Years of School, Brazil, 1948 and 1958.... 111

V–3. Level of Educational Attainment by Occupational Class of Father, Buenos Aires, 1960–1961.............. 115

V–4. Social-Class Origins of Students in Three Institutions of Higher Education, Brazil, *circa* 1955 (percentage distribution).. 118

V-5. Data on Educational Orientations of People with Higher Education, Argentina, 1946–1956 and 1956–1960, and Peru, 1950–1960 119

CHAPTER I

Defining Development

When American servicemen overseas dream of an end to conflict and their return home, they usually envision the United States as a true land of milk and honey. It is a place where one can order a thick milk shake, where one can easily get a car and the gas to run it, where meat on the table is a possibility at nearly every meal, where clothes can be easily bought and easily cleaned, and where sheets on the bed are the norm for nearly everyone. In other words, they consider America superior to the areas in which they are fighting or have fought (such as southern Europe, North Africa, Korea, Vietnam) mainly because its material wealth vastly outdistances most of the lands with which they have come in contact. The GIs have coined derogatory terms for the poor Asians, the poor North Africans, and others. But wealthy Americans of Asian parentage are exempt from this ignoble nomenclature because they have gained much of the material wherewithal that seems to remove the stigma.

In more academic language, we have come to call most of these countries and peoples falling outside Europe, North America, and Australia simply "underdeveloped" or, more hopefully, "developing." In recent years, interest has grown in the various social sciences concerning the reasons that might explain why some countries have become developed while others have not.

Historical Views of Development

Of course, certain Western social thinkers had considered the problem of development in the past, particularly in the eighteenth and early nineteenth centuries. However, the question was given little attention in the late nineteenth and the early twentieth centuries as other problems pressed for resolution. The exigencies of

1

war, urbanization, depression, inflation, political tyranny, and economic monopoly were in the forefront. The problem of continuing poverty did not loom large until after World War II, when many of the peoples of Africa, Asia, and Latin America became independent (or at least more aggressive on the world scene) and sometimes toyed with ideologies that seemed threatening to the relatively more favored countries of Europe and North America.

Looking back, we see that the problem of underdevelopment was of deep concern in the era when the European countries were just beginning to gain the momentum that would finally carry them into sustained development. The farther along the path they progressed, the less the problem of development itself was heeded. Other problems took precedence. Just as second-generation people of wealth spend little time in contemplating how they got rich and much time with the problems of managing and spending their money, so the West tended to forget the process by which it became relatively developed and was more concerned with the managing and utilization of its much increased resources. But thinkers in the earlier days of Western development were closer to the problem, and saw clearly many of the variables which were facilitating or impeding the further advance of their societies.

In England, from the middle of the eighteenth to the middle of the nineteenth century, a number of writers investigated and clarified the problems accompanying a process of social change that catapults a whole society toward development. Those whose ideas have had the greatest impact and whom we can still consider with profit are the so-called classical economists. Perhaps the most influential of these writers was Adam Smith, who published, in 1776, *An Inquiry into the Nature and Causes of the Wealth of Nations*. In this work, Smith saw the key to development in a rapid increase in the specialization of labor. But such specialization could not proceed without a concurrent increase in capital equipment with which to work, and an adequate fund by which the worker's necessities of life could be supplied. Also, the area in which the products of specialized labor could be marketed had to be widened, and obstacles to such trade reduced. Smith did not dwell on the social attitudes necessary for the development process. He simply assumed that men had an inborn tendency to barter and trade, and would carry the process forward once the external obstacles to specialization and free trade were removed. The idea that cultural influences were highly variable factors and far from natural and genetic did not receive much attention among classical economists. However, one of them—Malthus— did contend that people who did not *desire* to have more than the meanest way of life would assuredly not progress to any life beyond the most miserable.

David Ricardo, who wrote in the early years of the nineteenth century, was sure that the *sine qua non* of development was a distribution of wealth that assured the investing class (which ordered the capital equipment and accumulated funds sufficient to pay manufacturing labor enough to live) a share sufficient to sustain development. However, he believed there was a tendency for a growing population to increase food and therefore rent prices, thus shifting resources from the investing class to landlords. He did not have much hope that the investors' share would remain adequate for the long run, but he did hope that it might remain sufficient to support progress for at least a number of generations. For Europe and certain other areas, his pessimism turned out to be quite misplaced, but there are regions where a Ricardian pessimism today might be unhappily close to the mark.

Thomas Robert Malthus, whose famous work on population went through many editions from 1798 to 1830, considered permanent and uninterrupted progress in society impossible due to the tendency of men to procreate at a rate that would, in the very long run, create insurmountable obstacles to continued development. Moreover, men could reduce their rate of increase only by introducing practices that would sap what, to Malthus, was a main motive of human action—namely, the spur that men feel to work and create in order to support their offspring. Like Ricardo, and for somewhat similar reasons, Malthus was pessimistic about long-run development. When we look at European history we can see that his pessimism about population increase was over-drawn, and his views on human motivation seem doubtful. But the population problem in much of the non-European world seems to suggest that Malthus did locate an obstacle to development that may be the most intractable of all.

To these English classical economists, there was an unstated premise that social progress was, in essence, an economic problem. That is to say, the main question was: How do nations and their people become wealthier? Political factors and other aspects of society were considered chiefly with regard to their effects on the ability of society to accumulate capital and produce goods at a rate faster than the increase of the numbers in the society. The hinge upon which all development turned was economic progress.

Other writers of the time were not quite so willing to see social progress in such a stark economic framework. To such writers as Sismondi, a Swiss, and Saint-Simon, a Frenchmen, the role of the state and the spirit of the people were more than fixed factors or negative and secondary variables. Sismondi thought that progress depended on a social organization in which workers had steady opportunity and valid reasons to look toward their own advancement. The mass of people could not progress if they lost heart as impersonal "hands" in giant enterprise. Saint-Simon saw progress as dependent on the shift of the governing and managing function from backward feudal personalities to modern-minded entrepreneurs.

Current Development Terminology and Description

In our time, many of the issues of the early days of European development have again come to the forefront as the problem of worldwide development has engaged the energies of more and more students of society.

The idea of "development" is quite similar to the older concepts of "progress" or "advancement," and there has been some effort to give the concept greater precision. A society may change in a number of ways. It may become richer, more peaceable, and less authoritarian; or poorer, more peaceable, and more authoritarian; or richer, less peaceable, and more authoritarian; and so on. The list of characteristics could be greatly expanded, as could the combinations of possible change. Virtually no one would deny that "development" is a kind of social change during which the wealth and income of the society markedly increase. Some would argue that not only must the wealth available to society increase but this increase must be reflected in higher average incomes for the families and persons within that society. After all, wealth in a society can be largely given over to collective projects such as pyramid building, huge war expenditures, or ceremonial magnificence. Others would contend that social change, which is in truth "development," must include some liberalization of the political and ideological structure. Without some such liberalization, it might be argued, long-term increases in a society's wealth and per person income cannot be sustained or perhaps would not be worth having. The term "modernization," since it implies a wider and more interrelated complex of changing factors, sometimes is utilized as a substitute for the word "development." Some have attempted to make the idea of development more discrete by adding modifiers such as "economic" or "political" or "educational" or "ideological." This divisive approach, however, has limitations reminiscent of the old story of the blind men describing the elephant—the one who touches the trunk thinking it is like a snake, the one who touches the leg thinking it is like a tree.

In spite of the lack of consensus on the nature of development in the abstract sense, a perusal of the literature on the underdeveloped societies discloses a certain consistency in the descriptions advanced. If a country has many characteristics commonly noted as typical of underdevelopment, then, on general empirical grounds, one might consider it as an example of "underdevelopment." Often-mentioned characteristics of underdeveloped countries include the following:

1. High birth and death rates (but often with death rates declining and a consequent 2 to 3 per cent growth in population).
2. Poor sanitation and health practices (great lack of health services).
3. Poor housing.
4. High percentage of population in agriculture.

5. Low per capita income (and high percentage amount of this income for food).

6. Low food intake.

7. High illiteracy and very low enrollment in schools (particularly secondary and higher schools).

8. Weak and uneven feelings of national cohesion.

9. Tradition-directed behavior and an ascribed system of stratification.

10. Low status for women.

11. Poor technology (communication and transport systems limited).

12. High prevalence of child labor.

13. Export of raw materials in any foreign trade arrangements.

14. Low savings and low net investment.

15. Poor yield on the land and much soil depletion.

16. Military or feudal domination of state machinery.

17. Wealth in hands of landlords (a very tiny class as a proportion of the population) and the absence of a middle class.

18. Poor credit facilities and high interest rates.

19. Prevalence of nonmonetized production.

20. Much of the productive land in small holdings (often tenant-held).

21. Wealth concentrated in one or two large cities (or exported to "safe" developed countries).

22. Social loyalties and concern mainly family-centered or local in focus.

This list includes some of the most striking characteristics of societies that people have come to call underdeveloped. Of course, some societies which are generally considered developed may be characterized by one or another of the items on the list; and some underdeveloped countries are not well characterized by some of the features listed.

There is little question that low income is implied as at least a partial explanation for many items on the list; but such non-economic factors as traditional social structure, conservative value system, and political incapacity are also involved.

Modern Theories of Development

Rostow versus the Marxian View

A number of schemes for describing and analyzing the process of development have been evolved in recent years. One interesting effort to divide development into stages was devised by Walt W. Rostow, who rejects the Marxian progression from feudalism through commercial capitalism and monopolistic industrial capitalism to socialism and finally communism. Rather, his stages are the preindustrial, the "take-off," the mature, and the high mass consumption periods.

The key to Marx's scheme of economic stages was the shift in control of the means of production from one exploiting class to another. The new class of capitalists replaced the old traditional feudal land nobility. The capitalist stage then found the dominant class controlling the tools of industrial society and extracting its profits by garnering surplus value, or value created by labor but not paid to labor. But the constant addition of capital supposedly reduced the relative labor component of production, causing a fall in surplus value and the profits tied to it. The fall in profit then was to end the ability of the capitalist class to continually expand the capital component of production. Crisis, in the form of economic depression and increasing concentration of wealth and mass misery, would usher in a socialized stage that would finally evolve into a classless order.

Rostow agrees with Marx that a new and rising class, or elite, is necessary to move society into a new stage. He differs from Marx in that he argues that the development process does not inevitably generate crisis and misery. On the contrary, in the final stages of development, high mass consumption assures the masses a very comfortable material life. Whether the development process occurs under so-called capitalist conditions or under so-called socialist conditions is not of great interest to Rostow. He does feel, however, that Communist totalitarian political regimes are a likely disease of the period when an economy has taken off, but has not yet achieved maturity. Such regimes may slow the process of development, or they may not, but they are an unfortunate and unnecessarily high payment for developing people to make. To Rostow the key to the realization of development is simply a set of social circumstances which allows a continual large net investment accompanied by "approximate rationality" on the part of the investors or managers. Also needed are an expansion of technology and a sizable and varied market. As Rostow notes, his view is a "return to a rather old-fashioned way of looking at economic development.... What this argument does assert is that the rapid growth of one or more new manufacturing sectors is a powerful and essential engine of economic transformation."[1]

Under Marxist theory some but not all characteristics of underdeveloped countries are transformed by capitalism. Production is vastly increased and traditional behavior is obliterated; loyalties and family life are transformed; feudal domination is ended. But wealth remains concentrated, education is retarded, health and welfare services are advanced only to a minimal degree; and worst of all, the exploitive, increasingly irrational, and tyrannical hold of the owners of the means of production is maintained. However, to Rostow, the high mass consumption society seemingly transforms nearly *all* of the features that characterize a typical underdeveloped society.

Both Marx and Rostow see economic change, particularly capital expansion, as the key to progress. But Marx makes this expansion the result of an inexorable class conflict situation, while Rostow considers it the result of the fortunate emergence of an elite willing to apply technology to nature and do so in a relatively rational way. Political, familial, and religious questions are made part of the superstructure—not the basic keel of development—in Marx. In Rostow, these factors may influence the possibility of take-off and also the sustainment of development, but they will do so positively only if they evolve in a way favorable to economic transformation. Rostow and Marx agree in thinking of development as primarily an economic problem.

---

[1] Walt W. Rostow, "The Take-off Into Self-Sustained Growth," *Economic Journal,* Vol. LXVI (March 1956), p. 47.

Empirical Educational Development

Certainly most modern writing is in accord with economic emphasis in development. It is quite unlikely that many people would use the word "development" to apply to a society that was poor and getting poorer, but achieving greater political freedom, or greater religious fervor, or greater national solidarity. Some have used educational advance as a standard of development, but because it has a high correlation with improved GNP per capita, such a standard tends to measure the degree of economic growth as well as educational advance. One interesting effort to measure development on the basis of educational progress was worked out by Harbison and Myers. Seventy-five countries were divided into four stages of educational development. The criterion for the placement of countries in the four stages was worked out by computing a second-level enrollment ratio for each country (per cent of population aged 15–19 in school), which was adjusted for structural differences in secondary and postsecondary school organization arrangements in different countries.[2] This was weighted by one. Unadjusted third-level enrollment ratios (per cent of population aged 20–24) were computed, weighted arbitrarily by five, and added to the adjusted second-level enrollment ratio to get a composite index of educational development. The four stages were then delimited by this composite index, the arbitrary division being at 10, 32, and 75 on the index. Data on GNP per capita (about 1958) showed that level I (seventeen educationally underdeveloped countries) had a mean of $84; level II (twenty-one partially developed countries) had a mean of $182; level III (twenty-one semiadvanced countries) had $380; and level IV (sixteen advanced countries) had $1,100.

The implication of the Harbison and Myers scheme is that development necessarily involves educational advance as well as economic growth. The relationship is not determined, and it may be that economic growth simply brings in its wake more formal education. On the other hand, it is possible that educational de-

[2] Frederick H. Harbison and Charles A. Myers, *Education, Manpower, and Economic Growth* (New York: McGraw-Hill, 1964), pp. 23–48.

velopment is, in many cases, a necessary condition for further
economic development. The latter possibility directs one's attention to an assessment of development as a multifaceted phenomenon in which there is no one crucial element. Economic,
political, educational, familial, and religious factors may be so
inextricably intertwined that one cannot properly view economic
growth as the sole engine of development.

Social Differentiation

An effort to analyze development in the widest possible social
context has been advanced by Talcott Parsons and Neil Smelser
in a number of works, some jointly authored, others not.

According to their scheme, the process of development necessarily involves social differentiation. This means that the functions that all societies must constantly perform are accomplished
by social entities which become more and more specialized as a
society develops. In a simple, undeveloped society, the extended
family may be charged with satisfying most crucial social needs,
such as finding and distributing food and other goods, making
decisions concerning crime and punishment, making war, according honors, training the young, and the like. But in a more developed society such as the United States, a great specialization of
human institutional organization is evident. Special groups, such
as business firms, make and distribute food and other goods; yet
other social entities such as schools, governments, courts, and
professional organizations are engaged in performing highly
specific and crucial social functions. Thus, an undeveloped society is characterized by multifunctional institutions, while a developed society is one in which institutions become more and
more specialized and unifunctional in terms of meeting the problems of the society.

Usually new social structures oriented to a specialized social
function come into being because older, less specialized patterns of
meeting social needs have failed to adjust adequately to changed
conditions. Strains in the social order arising from changed conditions call forth new and more specialized ways of meeting the
crucial problems of society. Such strains may have been caused

by any number of historical trends, either internal or external to the social system. A change in geographical conditions, or a change in the nature of contacts with other social systems, is an example of external factors that may give rise to the beginnings of new concrete institutional structures within a social system. A new invention, either moral or physical, or a changing demographic variable, such as birth or death patterns or migration, exemplify internal factors that may create pressures which influence positively the coming of new and less multifunctional structures. For instance, the interpretation of general rules of behavior as they relate to particular actions may come to be the goal of a specific social structure such as the legal system. This means the transference of control away from a multifunctional institution, such as the family, to a specialized legal institution. For this to occur in any permanent sense, there must be a change in basic social values so that this new and specialized structure is made legitimate. Out of the old basic social values must come a new and more specific set of beliefs that support and guarantee the continuance of the new structure.

The whole process of development in the Western world over the past few centuries has been a continual specialization of new concrete social structures to more or less single social functions, and a concomitant reduction in the number of concrete structures with multifunctional aspects. As this process has accelerated, the general pattern of values has provided decreasing support for the continuation of concrete social structures that cannot be located primarily in limited functional categories. People have become disenchanted with institutions that still maintain important liaisons with more than one function, and the ongoing differentiation of social structure has continually become legitimatized and reinforced in the cultural values.

In this highly abstract view of development, the emphasis is not on economic growth as opposed to other factors, nor is economic growth the sole determining engine of development. Rather, the focus is on the interaction of elements within the social system in a way that creates conditions for the proliferation of specialized institutional structures. This view implies that economic growth may at some periods be an initiator of differentiation and at other

times a consequence of other factors creating change in the social
system. In this theory, an underdeveloped society is one in which
equilibrium is maintained within the rubric of a few undifferen-
tiated social structures. In such a situation continued economic
growth is highly unlikely. Some economic growth, however, may
set up strains in the social system which will facilitate differentiation. And this, in its turn, may encourage a long-run advance in
economic growth. Smelser's discussion of differentiation in religious systems illustrates the general orientation of this approach
to development:

> In the early phases of development, for instance, many tradi-
> tional loyalties may have to be broken in order to set up more dif-
> ferentiated social structures. Because these established commit-
> ments and methods of integration are deeply rooted in the
> organization of traditional society, a very generalized and power-
> ful value commitment is often required to "pry" individuals from
> these attachments. The values of ascetic and this-worldly religious
> belief, xenophobic national aspiration, and political ideologies
> such as socialism provide such a lever . . . . Insofar as they [reli-
> gious and nationalistic values] encourage the break-up of old pat-
> terns, they may stimulate economic development; insofar as they
> resist their own subsequent secularization, however, the very same
> values may become a drag on economic advance and structural
> change.[3]

Vicious Circle and Beneficent Circle Theories of Development

Some writers have concentrated on the self-sustaining difficulties facing the now underdeveloped countries. It is argued that
those who would put these countries on the development path
must realize that mutually supporting obstacles stand in the way.
Development in this case is seen essentially as what happens once
the elements that constitute the vicious circle are overcome. This
view is similar to the take-off metaphor found in Rostow's writings or the concept of differentiation central to the analyses of

[3]Neil J. Smelser, *The Sociology of Economic Life* (Englewood Cliffs, N.J.:
Prentice-Hall, 1963), p. 109. Smelser speaks of "economic" development, or
economic advance, to distinguish what happens in one part of the social system
from general social differentiation, which he sometimes calls "modernization" and
occasionally just "development" or "social development."

Parsons and Smelser. Once the vicious circle is broken, a beneficent circle takes over, pushing the society on toward "developed"
status.

Ragnar Nurske concentrated on the vicious circle of the small
market which limits productivity. In turn, this low productivity
limits the size of the market. He pointed to low capital formation
and low domestic saving as causes for low productivity, which is
a partial cause for a limited domestic market. Production for
foreign markets is often unfavorable for underdeveloped countries since undue concentration on one or two products fails to
create a spread of capital projects which are complementary in
"the sense that they provide a market for, and thus support, each
other." [4] Nurske argues that judicious efforts to control foreign
trade in the interests of balanced growth are a possible way out of
the deadlock.

Nurske builds his vicious-circle theory around such economic
variables as capital shortage, lack of markets, lack of synchroni-
zation of investment, foreign investment and trade factors, and
low saving incentives. The noneconomic factors are assumed to
be amenable to change as basic economic problems are solved
and an upward spiral of favorable economic relations creates a
developed society.

Gunnar Myrdal also argues that the problem of development
lies in the breaking of the vicious circle which derives primarily
from the fact that great regional economic inequalities, while accelerating gains in the richer areas, tend to create conditions that
continually widen the gap between regions. The best or, at least,
the younger people migrate to the expanding centers, and capital
finds its greatest return there. More human and capital resources
allow more adequate public financing of schools, health services,
and other basic social services. This process, however, leaves the
poorer areas with a smaller base for social services and a less productive age and talent structure. In underdeveloped countries,
the areas of advance do not spread out rapidly enough to offset
the retrogression occurring in the poorer regions. Myrdal argues:

[4] Ragnar Nurske, "Some International Aspects of the Problem of International
Development," *American Economic Review* (May 1952), p. 571.

If we use such a simple measure of regional inequality as the proportion of the total population of a country living in regions where the average income is less than two-thirds of the national average, we find that this proportion amounted to only a few per cent in Great Britain and Switzerland, to some ten per cent in such countries as Norway and France, and to about one-third in Italy, Turkey and Spain.... As a rule the free play of the market forces in a poor country will work powerfully to create regional inequalities and to widen those which already exist.... This is one of the interlocking relations by which in the cumulative process "poverty became its own cause."[5]

Not only regional but international market forces tend to create more wealth in the wealthy countries and greater poverty in the poor, and the "spread" effects of advance from advanced countries are too weak to overcome the inherent tendencies of the poor to move backward. According to Myrdal, breaking the cycle requires a more equal balance of power. Internationally, a greater bargaining power for the poor nations is needed. Domestically, a policy of state direction to assure the poor regions capital projects and social services is requisite to prevent their regressing in the face of the "natural" advantages of the few prosperous regions. Development cannot be expected under a regime of watch-and-wait. Positive state action in the underdeveloped countries is essential to redress the vicious circle of imbalance at home and abroad.

Another pattern of thinking about development in the vicious and beneficent circle tradition is that of Harvey Leibenstein. It is his view that the major obstacle to sustained development is likely to be the population problem. A small stimulant to increased production will only bring about somewhat improved health conditions, and some tendency for increased consumption among the mass of peasants, resulting in a population increase. However, the likelihood of decreasing returns must be considered. Thus, the growth in population may wipe out the gains made through the introduction of a new discovery or technique. The vicious circle can be broken if the initial stimulus to production

[5]Gunnar Myrdal, *Rich Lands and Poor* (New York: Harper, 1957), pp. 33–34.

is large enough to "generate an explosive income path."[6]   As
Leibenstein sees it:

> If the magnitude of the stimulant is "large," the outcome could
> readily be the reverse. The initial much larger increase in yield can
> now be sufficiently large to allow for (*a*) the initial increase in the
> peasant's consumption level; (*b*) the investments required for
> subsequent increases in the peasant's consumption level; (*c*) the
> increased yields necessary to take care of the autonomous and/or
> induced population growth; and (*d*) a sufficient increase in yield
> to permit some of the land to lie fallow to prevent soil depletion or
> to permit crop rotation.[7]

Development will occur only if the initial stimulus is above a
certain "minimal effort." If it is this large, a beneficent cycle of
events (growing income that will allow a greater proportional and
absolute saving, and will depress birth rates through education
and urbanization) will take over and guarantee an upward course.
In Leibenstein's words, "The minimum effort idea is both consistent with the vicious circle notion and at the same time offers a
way out."[8] The need is not so much for balanced investment, as
Nurske argues, or for balanced distribution of regional and international resources, as Myrdal contends; rather, a striking and
rapid improvement in production is required to overcome the
persistent income-depressing factors.

Summary

Development has captured much attention from social thinkers and social scientists in the past two decades. The growing dis-
parity between the well-being of most people in the developed
countries and the great masses in the underdeveloped lands, the
ideological struggle with Communist theory with its promises of
rapid progress, and the ending of colonialism have created a burst
of concern for both theory and action to transform the underdeveloped world.

[6]Harvey Leibenstein, *Economic Backwardness and Economic Growth* (New
York: Wiley, 1963), p. 99.
[7]*Ibid.*, p. 97.
[8]*Ibid.*, p. 98.

What is wanted is social change, but the change must be in the desired direction. It must represent what the nineteenth century termed "progress." The word "development," as applied to the social (or, more narrowly, the economic) context, involves a value judgment. In most discussions, the word "development" has replaced the word "progress," and the term "underdeveloped" has replaced the expression "backward." This has created a tendency to view the problem in an evolutionary frame of mind. One philosopher has argued that history justifies nothing, but that much of what has happened in history surely stands in need of justification. Thus, the Marxist approach, which introduces a specious determinism into historical change, need not be emulated in present-day thinking about the development problem. Societies are not wholly analogous to biological organisms. There is no inherent vital force in a society that automatically transforms it if some few objective conditions are fulfilled. We speak of the "developing societies," and of a "developing child." But there is a gulf between these two kinds of development. The child will develop into a man, or it will die. A society, however, may change in one direction for a time, then stop, and later revert more or less to its original condition. It has no absolutely set course.

We are not comitted to a position that it is bad to be a little boy and good to develop into an old man. This just happens. But we *are* committed to the idea that societies that are not "developed" are unfortunate and that it would be a good thing if they could become developed. Further, as Myint observes, there is a danger in the "underdevelopment" approach in that it tends to amalgamate people with natural resources, both being considered as underdeveloped.[9] The older emphasis on the "niggardliness of nature," when considered in relation to man's wants, is thus changed to an emphasis on man as a resource himself whose potential as a unit of production can unfold just as the iron ore in the mountain can be transmuted into tools. The question then becomes: What is the most efficient way of organizing

[9]H. Myint, "An Interpretation of Economic Backwardness," in A. N. Agarwala and S. P. Singh, eds., *The Economics of Underdevelopment* (New York: Oxford University Press, 1963), pp. 93–96.

efforts to speed this transformation of men and natural resources so that total output can be increased? But this question does not fully encompass the nature of the difficulty on which so much attention has been focused. A better statement of the problem would be: How can the way of life of people and the amount of economic goods available to them be changed so that a more satisfactory pattern of life emerges? The mere growth of production obviously does not imply a complete answer to the latter question.

> It does not necessarily follow that any efficient development of natural resources resulting in an increase in total output will always and *pari passu* reduce the backwardness of people . . . . Backwardness in many countries has been made more acute, not because the natural resources have remained "underdeveloped," but because they have been as fully and rapidly developed as market conditions permitted while the inhabitants have been left out, being either unable or unwilling, or both to participate fully in the process.[10]

The implication here is that people must be thought of, not as underdeveloped factors of production, but rather as mutable human beings whose presently backward way of life must be transformed so that better relationships between man and nature, and man and man, can be accomplished. The basic problem is not the status of the resources themselves. The development of natural resources is likely to be a necessary but not a sufficient means of solving the problem of human misery, degradation, and discontent.

The most reasonable approach to development is to be quite candid about the value judgments one is making. Perhaps one reason for the shift from such words as "advanced" and "backward" or "progressive" and "unprogressive" was that these terms were too invidious, too derogatory, too obviously frank. But little is gained if an inordinate lack of clarity is introduced into the discussion because of a wish to be more polite. We think it *is* better for most people to live under the conditions that are typical in Scandinavia, for example, than it is for them to live in the pattern that exists in, say, India, Peru, or Nigeria. The ap-

[10] *Ibid.*, p. 96.

proach that Parsons and Smelser take toward development seems promising. The whole structure of society must be changed. New institutions, new values, and new patterns of integration must be forthcoming. Objective models are needed, but models that deal solely with resource development (people being considered as resources along with nonhuman factors) are too restrictive and tend to take one's attention away from the problem of metamorphosing the way of life of the backward peoples of the world.

The concern in this book is to concentrate on the role of education in this metamorphosis. This involves a description of the present status and trends of formal education in the underdeveloped world. It also involves some reasoned generalizations about its potential role and the obstacles to the realization of this role. A consideration of the contribution of education to the already realized advances in the developed world may give some insights into the kinds of things that might be expected from the use of schools in bringing about desired social change. That great hopes exist for using education as a major lever to lift backward social orders to more satisfactory levels is evident from the statements and policies of governments throughout the world. A quotation from a recent Indian Government resolution, announcing a new education commission to study education at all levels, includes some comments that illustrate the expectations of leaders in the underdeveloped world for using education to change the social order:

> Greater emphasis came to be placed on educational development because of the realization that education, especially in science and technology, is the most powerful instrument of social transformation and economic progress; and that the attempt to create a new social order based on freedom, equality, and justice can succeed only if the traditional educational system was revolutionized both in content and extent.[11]

Given these hopes and the conscious use of education in schemes for desired social change, there is little question that planning of educational expansion and innovation will increase at

[11] *The Times of India* (Delhi, July 17, 1964), cited in John W. Hanson and Cole S. Brembeck, eds., *Education and the Development of Nations* (New York: Holt, Rinehart and Winston, 1966), pp. 344–345.

the national level. The educational changes which occurred in England and some other advanced societies came in fits and starts and were largely the result of somewhat fortuitous circumstances. On the other hand, in Japan and Russia, education has been used in a more conscious way to build a new social structure. It is likely that most underdeveloped societies will attempt to follow the example of the latter countries and will exert great effort to link their educational systems instrumentally with their national aims.

Suggested Readings for Chapter I

ALMOND, G. A., and J. S. COLEMAN, eds. *The Politics of the Developing Areas.* Princeton: Princeton University Press, 1960.

Council of World Tensions. *Restless Nations: A Study of World Tensions and Development.* New York: Dodd, Mead, 1962.

HARBISON, FREDERICK H., and CHARLES A. MYERS. *Education, Manpower, and Economic Growth.* New York: McGraw-Hill, 1964.

HEILBRONER, ROBERT L. *The Making of Economic Society.* Englewood Cliffs, N.J.: Prentice-Hall, 1962.

LEIBENSTEIN, HARVEY. *Economic Backwardness and Economic Growth.* New York: Wiley, 1963.

LEWIS, W. ARTHUR. *Development Planning: The Essentials of Economic Policy.* New York: Harper, 1966.

MYRDAL, GUNNAR. *Rich Lands and Poor.* New York: Harper, 1957.

PARSONS, TALCOTT, and NEIL SMELSER. *Economy and Society.* Glencoe, Ill.: The Free Press, 1956.

ROSTOW, WALT W. *The Stages of Economic Growth.* Cambridge: The University Press, 1960.

SMELSER, NEIL. *The Sociology of Economic Life.* Englewood Cliffs, N.J.: Prentice-Hall, 1966.

THEOBOLD, ROBERT. *The Rich and the Poor.* New York: Mentor, 1960.

WARD, BARBARA. *The Rich Nations and the Poor Nations.* New York: Norton, 1962.

The Contribution of Education to Development

In Chapter I we undertook the task of deciding what is meant by development. A number of different conceptions were surveyed, and some clarification was attempted. In the chapters to follow we shall examine education in three major developing regions of the world and identify certain educational problems common to less developed nations. The task of Chapter II is to go beyond description and analyze the ways education has contributed in the past, and theoretically might contribute in the future, to the development process.

Education in the Already Developed Societies

One possible approach to understanding the place of education in development is to look at its role in societies that have passed through the development process. By comparing the present state of education in the more developed societies with its place during the years when these societies were undergoing change, we may be afforded a few rewarding insights. Unfortunately, in this regard, lack of adequate information precludes investigation into many important areas. Yet there is enough material available to designate some significant regularities.

Most of the developed societies are in Europe or in areas settled by Europeans. Japan is, at present, the major exception. In all these countries the degree of literacy is very high, and the proportion of school-age children (6 to 15 years old) actually attending school approaches 100 per cent. Also, relatively high proportions of young people in their late teens and early twenties are in secondary schools or higher educational institutions. Is this fact of central or only peripheral importance for the continued existence of these societies in a developed stage? It is our contention that the level of education in these societies is among the most important elements that explain the maintenance of societies in a developed form. A few of the many arguments which could be put forth to support this observation are now considered.

First, in developed societies, production and trade are almost wholly monetized. This implies a vast system of abstract bookkeeping, information gathering and storing, complex contractual arrangements, general comprehension of numerical relationships, and so on. The proportion of the people in these societies who simply could not perform any crucial social role without basic literacy and arithmetical ability has grown to include nearly everyone. The position of the unschooled person in developed societies is somewhat comparable to the situation a traveler would face in a foreign country if he did not know the language, and no one knew his.

Second, in these societies an extraordinarily large number of crucial communications are in written rather than oral form. Such an important social necessity as the allocation of labor is built around written want ads, employment records, written applications, letters of recommendation, government job opportunities reports, and so on. Factory rules, employment regulations, wage and hour laws, and myriads of written notices make life for the illiterate in these societies almost impossible. Even in households many essential areas of concern imply reading ability. Operating instructions, lists of ingredients, labels on foods and drugs, water and fuel bills, for example, are a part of the daily home life of nearly everyone in the developed countries.

Third, in the developed countries customary law and simple mores are completely unworkable, since political and economic organization demands a system of written law enforceable throughout the nation. The schools are major centers for the inculcation of a feeling of loyalty to the national symbols that support such a system. Moreover, literacy is very important to needed social adaptations, since the events that call for modifications in the system of written law are for the most part made known to the citizens through written communications.

Fourth, the dependence of the developed society on advanced technology is absolute. The fabric of society could be sustained in an underdeveloped nation even if the limited advanced technical processes should fall into disuse. In the developed societies, any major retreat from advanced technology would spell social disaster. The large urban masses in developed societies are dependent for their food and other necessities on their ability to command these things either from a technically-advanced agriculture in their own society or from abroad, by the trading power of goods produced by advanced techniques. The large number of people who must be able to manage and manipulate this technical apparatus tends to grow in developed societies. Basic education and, for many, higher schooling become indispensable in such a situation. The populations of the developed countries could certainly not be sustained under their present social and economic forms without a large and constant stream of technically competent people being trained in each generation. On this ground alone, education—far from being an interesting but secondary accompaniment of developed societies—is central to their very existence.

Fifth, no developed society can be maintained without some demographic balance. All developed societies, partly as a by-product of the basic technical advance that underlies their order, have seen their death rates drop to very low levels. They have also seen change in the older patterns of fertility. If the developed societies had maintained the fertility levels of predevelopment epochs, while at the same time maintaining the new low death rates, they would assuredly come to a point where they would have to revert in important ways to the underdevelopment pattern. Education is among the major forces bringing fertility rates down in the developed societies, and tends to reinforce the population's orientation toward the future. Since excessive fertility in the urban setting typical of developed societies carries many disadvantages for the individual family in the long run, the more future-oriented the people, the more prone they are to act, in order to reduce their potential fertility. Further, education often brings with it an enhanced sophistication regarding biological processes and knowledge of methods through which unwanted births can generally be prevented. Most demographers characterize the fertility situation in developed countries as "controlled." Without the high average schooling of the populations of these societies, it is doubtful whether the degree of fertility control would be as adequate as it is.

There are other reasons for considering education as a pivotal force in the maintenance of the presently advanced societies as developed social orders. However, from the standpoint of underdeveloped countries, there is a more interesting question: What role did educational advance play in the long process by which these societies transformed themselves into developed nations? It is, of course, possible that, although education is presently crucial to the developed societies, it played little or no part in beginning or accelerating the process of development. And it is also possible that even if education played little part in the advancement of the presently developed world, it may still be of great significance in the development process of the many societies now striving to break out of old patterns. The following sections will attempt an analysis of these questions.

England. Development demands a sharp break with traditional forms of human interaction. It is not likely to occur unless serious strains in the social order require a reordering of deeply entrenched institutional patterns. In England, the first nation to experience the long-run process of development, discontent with the old order was centered in the dissenting groups who wished to purify the Church of England and reform the morals of the population. Such people in France and other countries on the Continent often suffered extreme isolation or expulsion, but in England the outcome of the Revolution of 1688 was to create a condition in which dissenting groups were allowed to follow their ways with minimal harassment. Many of these people became businessmen, involved in the growing industries of the north of England, where the textile trade was perhaps expanding most rapidly. Because of discontent with inefficient "putting-out" work assignments, the traditional dishonesty of workers, the lack of discipline in the working force, and the unavailability of labor, the shop masters became increasingly insistent upon change. Smelser comments that this dissatisfaction had to be based on the particular values held by the increasingly important business classes:

> Why were these institutional bottlenecks a source of dissatisfaction? Why did not the masters and workmen let well enough alone, particularly in good times? Why did the masters complain about deliveries on schedule? Why did they object to a loss of material through semitraditionalized theft and embezzlement? Could they not assume this as a "cost" to be met by stiffening their terms of exchange with the weavers? In short, what *values* made dissatisfaction with the existing state of affairs a legitimate and appropriate response?[1]

The values were to be found in the nonconformist doctrines to which a probable majority of the masters adhered or sympathized. The beliefs of these people led them to anathematize behavior that was undisciplined, irrational, unmethodical, extravagant, and slothful.

In the end, this discontent led to changed arrangements in the division of labor through new techniques that were rapidly accepted by the masters as a way out of an impasse. Also, an increasing number of workmen and the population in general accepted, in large part, the course of change. The beginning of the process of development was under way.

It is well known that the nonconformist groups in England were avid in their support of the advances of scientific and technical knowledge in the seventeenth and eighteenth centuries. Armytage[2] points out that dissenter academies in the eighteenth century were often staffed by Englishmen who, excluded from Oxford and Cambridge by the Act of Uniformity in 1662, trained in Scottish universities. The schools which they founded were more likely to study the new scientific experiments and their practical applications than were the older colleges and academies. Such devices as microscopes, magnets, optical cards, and "Electrifying Machines" were to be found in the dissenter academies.

---

[1] Neil J. Smelser, *Social Change in the Industrial Revolution* (Chicago: University of Chicago Press, 1959), pp. 66–67.

[2] W. H. G. Armytage, "Education and Innovative Ferment in England, 1588–1805," in C. Arnold Anderson and Mary Jean Bowman, eds., *Education and Economic Development* (Chicago: Aldine, 1965), pp. 390–391.

Experiment, as it was understood at the time, was highly regarded, and "from these academies came many of those who were to marry science and industry."

It was this drive to "marry science and industry" that culminated in the innovations that were cardinal to the transformation of English society. The practical bent of the education of the new and increasingly important business class acted to encourage new forms of production. New methods were much desired in order to overcome the traditional social forms that seemed to stand in the way of the material and ideal interests of this class.

During the preindustrial period of English history the universities were not sympathetic to the new knowledge that a cosmopolitan group of thinkers on the Continent and in England had fashioned. As a reaction to the disfavor of Oxford and Cambridge to experimental science and mathematics, a group of diverse personalities finally established a society "to improve the knowledge of all natural things, and in all useful Arts, Manufacture, Mechanick practices, Engynes and Inventions by Experiments—(not meddling with Divinity, Metaphysics, Moralls, Politics, Grammar, Rhetoric, or Logick)."[3] A poem (probably written by William Clanville) expressed the sentiments of the society toward their work and the traditional universities. According to the poem, the society wanted to "know all things by demonstration," and "Oxford and Cambridge are our laughter; their learning is but pedantry."[4] Many of the members of this new Royal Society (chartered in 1662) were drawn from the ranks of merchants, most without university learning. Robert Hooke's memoirs remark on this:

> Many of their [the Royal Society's] number are men of traffic which is a good omen that their attempts will bring philosophy from words to action, seeing that men of business have had such great share in the first foundation . . . . Several merchants, men

[3] C. R. Weld, *A History of the Royal Society with Memoirs of the Presidents, Compiled with Authentic Documents* (London: 1848). This passage was taken from the manuscript volume of Robert Hooke's papers, written in 1663; cited in Martha Ornstein, *The Role of Scientific Societies in the Seventeenth Century* (Chicago: University of Chicago Press, 1928), fn., pp. 108–109.

[4] *Ibid.*, p. 111.

who act in earnest, have adventured considerable sums of money to put in practice what some of our members have contrived.[5]

Thus, the learning of the class that was to be the catalyst of the development process in England was not typical of the traditional learning of the older and entrenched elite. It was not so much the level of the education of this sector of the population but its qualitatively different ethos that was so important in actuating the innovative behavior which contributed much to making Britain the leading nation on the road to modernization.

But what of the educational level of the mass of Englishmen in the period just before and after the take-off of English development? The data are fragmentary and scattered, but certain tentative generalizations are possible. For one thing, it does not appear that basic literacy or the number of schools per population improved much until the process of development was well advanced. Second, while universal literacy and basic mass education were deferred until the end of the nineteenth century, the level of English literacy was relatively high in the sixteenth and seventeenth centuries, especially as compared with many underdeveloped countries today. Third, the basis for widely spread formal education was laid some few decades after the beginning of the development process, as family units became less able to perform basic training and socialization functions under the factory system.

1. *The slow growth of basic literacy*

It is likely that somewhat over two-fifths of the English male population in the fifteenth and sixteenth centuries were literate. S. L. Thrupp estimated that 50 per cent of lay male Londoners in the fifteenth century could read English.[6] J. W. Adamson made an examination of jury lists during the middle period of the fifteenth century and noted that in Norfolk "in a group of men

[5]Robert Hooke, *Observations of the Late Eminent Dr. Robert Hooke, F.R.S. and Geom. Prof., and Other Eminent Virtuoso's of His Time* (London: W. Deham, F.R.S., 1726), preface. Cited in Ornstein, *op. cit.*, p. 111.

[6]S. L. Thrupp, *The Merchant Class of Medieval London* (Chicago: University of Chicago Press, 1948), pp. 157–171. Cited in C. Arnold Anderson, *Literacy and Schooling on the Development Threshold*, in Anderson and Bowman, *op. cit.*, p. 347.

drawn from widely separated social classes thirty-seven and a half per cent are styled literate."[7] He goes on to note that "much the same proportion occurs in a document of 1373 relating to a suit between William of Wykeham and the Masters of St. Cross, Winchester."[8] By the eighteenth century there had been some increase in the percentage of literacy. W. L. Sargent noted that "on the accession of George III (1760), 56 per cent of the towns-people, and 40 per cent of the country people, signed their names."[9] He also noted that at the time of Victoria's accession (1837) the figure for townspeople had changed little, while improvement had occurred among country people (from 40 per cent in 1760 to 60 per cent in 1837).[10]

As for schools, A. F. Leach worked out estimates of grammar schools per capita and put the figure at the time of the reign of Edward VI (*circa* 1550) at one grammar school to every 5,625 people; in a report of 1864, the figure was one to every 23,750.[11] These figures would imply that, even if basic education made some small advances in the two centuries before and the half-century after the beginning of development, more advanced instruction possibly became more limited on a per capita basis during the era leading up to and following the "take-off." In any case, it does not appear that any major forward strides were made in the education of the large mass of Englishmen in the years just preceding the great transformation, or for many decades thereafter.

2.   *The relatively high educational level of the English people in the predevelopment stage*

It should be remembered that the English people had reached a level of educational development (at least in basic literacy) by

[7] J. W. Adamson, "The Extent of Literacy in England," *The Library,* Ser. 4, 10: 166–168 (1929). Cited in Anderson, *op. cit.*, p. 348.

[8] *Ibid.*

[9] W. L. Sargent, "On the Progress of Elementary Education," *Royal Statistical Society Journal*, 30: 90–91 (1887). Cited in Anderson, *op. cit.*, p. 347.

[10] *Ibid.*

[11] A. F. Leach, *The Schools of Medieval England* (1915), p. 331. Cited in R. H. Tawney, *Religion and the Rise of Capitalism* (New York: Harcourt, Brace, 1926), fn., p. 255.

the sixteenth century that was probably much higher than most underdeveloped countries have achieved today. India, with some 20 per cent of the underdeveloped world's people, cannot claim much more than about 18 per cent literacy; much of Africa and the Middle East are as low as or lower than India on this measure. The underdeveloped countries today that have reached or surpassed English predevelopment levels are often countries already clearly on the development path; Taiwan, Greece, Venezuela, Chile, and Cuba are examples.

3. *The reduction of the role of the family and the rise of mass education*

Between 1550 and 1650 the formal English elementary school probably came into wide use by the more favored classes who formerly had trained their children at home for grammar school.[12] But the extension of this system to the mass of people in England occurred almost three centuries later, from 1830 to 1910. Smelser hypothesized that the factory acts of the 1830's and 1840's had as their effect the separation of parents from children for much longer periods of the day. (The children had shorter hours prescribed and therefore often would not be hired along with parents after the passage of the acts.) With this separation, the mass of parents came to view schools as a necessary supplement of their relations with the children rather than as competitors for the children's time and services. Smelser points out that before the passage of the Factory Act of 1833, and particularly during the agitation for it in the 1820's, the leaders of the labor cause were not enthusiastic in support of formal education for the masses. But, surprisingly, the manufacturers were.

> [In England in the 1820's and 1830's] the enemies and defenders
> of the factory system, however, looked in different directions; the
> ten-hour men might look backward to the de-differentiated system
> of paternalistic responsibility of master or church, whereas their
> opponents looked forward to a family system and an educational
> system more differentiated than before. Indeed, it was the manu-

---

[12] Anderson and Bowman, *op. cit.*, p. 358.

facturers themselves who suggested the adoption of an embryonic sort of formal educational system for the Act of 1833.[13]

After the Act of 1833 there was an irreversible change in the general values of the mass of parents. If the child worked, he could not put in coextensive hours with his parents, and would also receive schooling with or without the parents' option. If the employer decided not to hire children because of the stipulation of the law, an even greater estrangement of children from parents would ensue. This, too, would bend the parents' sentiments to the side of those who supported formal schooling for children. Smelser points out that the Act canceled the older parental options of deciding whether to work the child or send him to school.

> If the Act, by restricting the child's hours of labor, removed him from his adults' care on the factory premises, it seemed natural to re-establish on another basis some of the responsibilities it took from the parents.[14]

It appears, then, that a separate system of formal education (elementary) appeared in the preindustrial stage, but that the base for its tremendous expansion to the mass of people occurred only many decades after English development had begun.

The role of formal elementary education in initiating English development was far less significant than the qualitatively different kind of higher learning acquired by the rising business and technical classes in the predevelopment stage. This nontraditional education was instrumental in resolving a number of problems involved in the early period of social strain present in the beginning of development. But to ensure the continuance of the development process, England, in the middle and late nineteenth century, moved toward universal elementary schooling as a means for transmitting indispensable values to the young. The circumstances which assisted in the extension of basic education were, as has been mentioned, the reforming impulses that brought into being the factory acts. Moreover, after their passage, universal state education was seen as a necessary concomitant of these acts.

[13] Smelser, *op. cit.,* p. 287.
[14] *Ibid.,* p. 295.

Pipkin emphasizes the close tie between government efforts to limit the hours worked in factories (particularly by children) and extended education:

> Education was made the motive and object of restricting children's hours of work, and then the factory inspectors in their turn became promoters or furtherers of state education, because they realized that only thereby could the restriction of hours become effective. From 1870 to 1921 some twenty-three Acts ... contributed to build up the public system in England.[15]

It is clear that traditional values were securely lodged in English higher education during the earlier stages of the development process. Indeed, during this period, English universities were less amenable to change than were institutions of higher learning in the countries that later went through the development process. The first chair of engineering was established in the University of Glasgow in 1840. Cambridge had no chair of engineering until 1875. It took the shock of the International Exhibition of 1867 to alter British higher education in ways that would accelerate the process of development. In the Exhibition of 1851, British products were still preeminent, but in Paris, in 1867, British products received few awards. British industrial supremacy had obviously been effectively challenged by other countries. A government committee found education defective at all levels in Britain in that it failed to adequately train scientists, technologists, and industrial managers. The committee recommended

> ... elementary instruction within reach of every child, elementary science as an ingredient of all schooling, the reorganization of some secondary schools as science schools, State support for "superior colleges of science" to be established in centers of industry, the encouragement of education for higher science teachers "by granting of degrees in science at Oxford and Cambridge."[16]

With this impetus, science, if not technology, made slow headway in English universities during the last half of the nineteenth century. Higher technology, if excluded from Oxford and Cam-

[15] Charles W. Pipkin, *Social Politics and Modern Democracies* (New York: Macmillan, 1958), pp. 68–69.
[16] Sir Eric Ashby, *Technology and the Academies* (London: Macmillan, 1958), p. 59.

bridge, did become entrenched in the seven new colleges that were established between 1871 and 1881 (Newcastle, Leeds, Bristol, Birmingham, Sheffield, Liverpool, and Nottingham). In the end, technology finally became a part of the curriculum of the traditional centers, Oxford and Cambridge. It was, and is to this day, a difficult transition as technologists are really only tolerated in universities because government and business underwrite their activities: "Tolerated but not assimilated; for the traditional don is not yet willing to admit that technologists may have anything intrinsic to contribute to academic life." [17]

The difficulty of fitting ancient English traditions of higher education into the flow of development needs was reflected in a Fabian Tract written by George Bernard Shaw in 1901. In one section of the Tract, entitled, "Be Careful in Endowing Education," Shaw advised millionaires not to give their money to institutions out of tune with the development process:

> An intelligent millionaire, unless he is frankly an enemy of the human race, will do nothing to extend the method of caste initiation practiced under the mask of education at Oxford and Cambridge. Experiments in educational method, and new subjects of technical education ... or economics, statistics, and industrial history, treated as part of the technical commercial education of the wielder of modern capitals and his officials; these, abhorrent to university dons and outside the scope of public elementary education, are the departments in which the millionaire can make his goal fruitful.... It is the struggles of society to adapt itself to the new conditions which every decade of modern industrial development springs on us that need help. The old institutions, with their obsolete routine, and their lazy denials and obstructions in the interests of that routine, are but too well supported already.[18]

Japan[19]

The development process in Japan occurred under different conditions from those that prevailed in England, and, once

[17] *Ibid.*
[18] George Bernard Shaw, *Socialism for Millionaires* (London: The Fabian Society, Fabian Tract No. 107, July 1901), p. 10.
[19] Much of this discussion on Japan is drawn from Donald K. Adams' and Robert M. Bjork's "Modernization as Affected by Governmental and International Educational Influences: Japan," in *Governmental Policy and International Education*, Stewart Fraser, ed. (New York: Wiley, 1965), pp. 269–294.

begun, the rapidity of the transformation of Japanese economic and political life was much greater.

The period between 1850 and 1875 marked the beginning of the Japanese development process. The stage was set for basic change when serious strains in the fabric of Japanese society began to appear as early as the late eighteenth century and the political and cultural unity of the Tokugawa period (1603–1867) began to dissolve. In part, this dissatisfaction was due to the increasing awareness of part of the upper strata concerning Western military and technical prowess.

Examples of this tendency are seen in the career of certain Japanese scholars. For example, Takano Choei and Katsu Rintaro studied Western ideas through the medium of the Dutch language. Such scholars condemned the policy of the Tokugawa shogunate in resisting the introduction of Western learning, wrote memorials highly critical of Japanese military organization, and proposed schools in which Japan's diplomats and military men could be trained in Western procedures. The ferment of the first few decades of the nineteenth century resulted in the founding of a school for the study of the Dutch language in 1838 and an Institute for the Study of Barbarian Writings in 1855.

During the century preceding the beginning of Japanese development, there was a growing challenge to traditional higher schooling in Japan. Just as scientific societies and dissenter academies challenged the traditional learning of Oxford and Cambridge in England, a number of higher schools were established by powerful feudal clans. The major institution of higher learning in Japan during the Tokugawa period was the Tokyo Shoheiko (School of Prosperous Peace), a center of orthodox Confucian scholarship, dominated by the ruling Tokugawa clan. The growth of competing clan schools was rapid in the late Tokugawa period, and there were 250 of them by 1850. Certain of these clan schools, such as the Mito and Satsuma, emphasized Japanese history and literature. They stressed the idea of a Japanese national destiny and the symbol of the Emperor in contrast to the Shoheiko, which remained firmly attached to Confucian classics and was not interested in nationalistic movements that might threaten the stability of Tokugawa rule. Lombard comments on the significance of these schools: "That there were men ready to lead in the restoration was due in large part to the influence of certain schools, notably that of Mito; and that there were men ready to welcome foreign association was also due to the work of certain independent teachers whose efforts kindled the foregleams of the second great awakening." [20]

Just as the dissenting religions in England tended to justify the dissatisfactions with traditional forms felt by the rising group of businessmen, a new philosophy performing the same function in Japan gained increased importance in the late Tokugawa period. This philosophy was known as Shingaku; and, while it accepted the moral and ethical principles found in Confucian writings, it also taught that knowledge divorced from action is sterile. In this philosophy, merchants were necessary to the society and were to be accorded respect. While urging economy and frugality as virtues, Shingaku argued that profits were as morally proper for the merchant as the stipend was for the samurai, or warriors. Thus, through the spread of these new views, a challenge was presented to the traditional view that merchants followed the least honorable of callings and should adhere to the virtues of obedience, deference, and poverty.

The influence of Western knowledge, the new nationalism of the clan schools, and the unorthodox challenges to Confucian dominance in philosophy all combined to create dissatisfaction with traditional social arrangement among the dissident elements of the upper and middle strata of society. As in England, it was not so much the level as the quality of higher learning that was important in helping initiate the development process.

The masses of Japanese people in the predevelopment stage were, of course, rural. The educational level of this great majority of the Japanese population improved as the Tokugawa era wore on, particularly after 1800.[21] By the end of the Tokugawa era, approximately 40 per cent of the boys and 15 per cent of the girls were attending school. Perhaps 40 per cent of the male population had become literate by the time of the Meiji restoration

---

[20] F. Lombard, *Pre-Meiji Education in Japan* (Tokyo: Kyo-Kwan, 1913), p. 90.
[21] See Herbert Passin, "Portents of Modernity and Meiji Emergence," in Anderson and Bowman, *op. cit.,* pp. 394–421.

(1868). The figure is much less for the females. Compared to the situation at the beginning of the Tokugawa period, this was a great improvement. It is not likely that in the early period (*circa* 1700) even a majority of the samurai were literate, much less the commoners. Thus, in some contrast with England, which did not experience any great improvement in literacy in the two centuries preceding development, Japan made large strides. However, the level to which Japanese literacy had moved by the beginning of the Meiji period was similar to the English level in the mid-eighteenth century. The spread of basic literacy in the Tokugawa era was associated with (1) a rapid increase in the domain of fief schools, which had begun to enroll commoners in addition to samurai, and (2) expansion of the Terakoya, or parishioners' schools, which were attended largely by commoners. These schools did not, for the most part, reflect the forces that were setting the stage for the transformation of Japanese society. Passin comments on the curriculum of the Terakoya:

> More advanced students might be assigned the simpler Confucian classics, such as the *Four Books*, and girls given some suitable Confucian work or Kaibara Ekken's improving tract for Samurai women, the *Greater Learning for Women* (Onna Daigaku). But these were the minority. For the overwhelming majority, the curriculum was basically the three R's plus some instruction in morals and manners.[22]

Formal elementary education spread rather slowly in England after development began, taking well over a century to become the norm for the whole population. In Japan, the process was accelerated. Within fifty years after the development process had begun, Japan had achieved universal formal primary education. The use of the elementary school to speed development was a much more conscious act in Japan than in England, and the Japanese had defined a scheme for compulsory education within a very few years after the Meiji restoration. The Education Law issued by the Department of Education in 1872 stated in its preamble:

> Every man only after learning diligently each according to his capacity will be able to increase his property and prosper in his

[22] *Ibid.*, p. 411

business. Hence knowledge may be regarded as the capital for raising one's self; who then can do without learning? ... It is intended that henceforth universally (without any distinction of class or sex) in a village there shall be no house without learning, and in a house no individual without learning.[23]

The Japanese educational authorities energetically moved to make the curriculum of elementary schools serve the ends of development. In the 1870's the Western approach to arithmetic, hygiene, and science was becoming entrenched in the elementary-school curriculum. Borrowing from the educational traditions of the West became a common practice. Particularly in the early Meiji period, Japan emphasized techniques for training teachers which were common to the American normal schools, and curricula, school equipment, and the general orientation of elementary schools were carbon copies of American schools. Many school items were imported from America, and American schoolbooks were translated and often used as the sole text material in the classroom.[24]

It is clear that the Japanese leaders expected and received from the rapidly expanding elementary schools a performance that helped to create values in accordance with the now rapidly changing Japanese society. The elementary schools extolled the new, but at the same time continued to emphasize precepts aimed at family discipline and stability. The inevitable difficulties that change presents to many people were moderated in Japan by the continued ability of the family to give some security, and to blunt tensions. The 1890 Imperial Rescript on Education, and earlier less famous proclamations, demanded that all citizens show reverence for ancestors, and filial piety. In the schools this document was read daily, and there are stories of teachers losing their lives in heroic attempts to rescue the Rescript from burning school buildings. To a surprising degree, such traditional support of family solidarity was combined rather successfully with an inculcation of values often considered to weaken family ties. Some of these were: a greatly increased acceptance of achievement of status unaffected by class, age, or even sex; an increased

---

[23] Kikuchi Dairoku, *Japanese Education* (London: J. Murray, 1909), pp. 68–69.
[24] Inazo Nitobe, *et al., Western Influences in Modern Japan* (Chicago: University of Chicago Press, 1931), p. 36.

regard for analytic rationality; and an upgrading of national, as opposed to local, symbols.

By 1900, the enforcement of four years of compulsory education was complete. And by 1908, just forty years after the beginning of the Meiji era, compulsory education had been effectively increased to six years. Perhaps more consciously than in any of today's developed countries, the new elite of Japan during the early period of development saw basic education as a crucial ingredient of rapid transformation. As a Ministry of Education publication of 1963 states:

> It is noteworthy that in the 30 years after the introduction of the modern school system, compulsory education was almost universally observed, and the general modernization of Japan was achieved in the same period; . . . it must be emphasized that the people as well as their leaders entertained great expectations of modern education and made utmost efforts for its development.[25]

Education in the Development of Today's Less Developed Societies

We have seen that the beginnings of development in such countries as England and Japan were tied to education by virtue of the fact that the "development-makers" came out of an educational milieu that was at odds with traditional patterns. It also seems that the general population had achieved a certain degree of literacy (perhaps 30 to 40 per cent) before the development process began, after which there was a shift in the training of children of the masses—from the home, clan, and church to a formal system of elementary schools. At the higher levels of education, old traditional ways in curricula and ethos gave way to educational forms more in accord with development needs. These changes were rapid in Japan, while they were slow and halting in Britain, but in the end a more or less complete transformation occurred in both countries.

Does this pattern contain any lessons for those who are consciously trying to bring about development in the underdeveloped world today? It seems evident that change will not occur in

[25] Ministry of Education, Government of Japan, *Japan's Growth and Education* (Tokyo: July 1963), pp. 32–33.

nations that do not have discontented elites who are committed to actions that will cause crucial alterations in the existing social equilibrium. In the past few decades increasing numbers from the upper and middle strata of underdeveloped countries have received higher education in the industrialized cultures, or in schools in their own countries run by Westerners. They often emerge with a determination to be a part of the modernization forces in their own societies. Certainly one of the key elements in the present ferment in the hitherto static societies has been the impact of Western education on a particular segment of the population. The commitment of these new elements to change has, of course, run into traditional opposition of greater or less intensity. When Smelser hypothesized that institutional differentiation is inherently associated with development, he observed that the continual need for reintegration brings a three-way tug-of-war as efforts are made to alter the old equilibrium:

> Such innovations are often opposed ... by traditional vested interests because the new forms of integration compete with the older, undifferentiated systems of solidarity. The result is a three-way tug-of-war among the forces of tradition, the forces of differentiation, and the new forces of integration .... Three classic responses to these discontinuities are anxiety, hostility, and phantasy. These responses, if and when they become collective, crystallize then into a variety of social movements—peaceful agitation, political violence, millenarianism, nationalism, revolution, underground subversion .... In many cases the beliefs are highly emotional and unconcerned with realistic policies.[26]

One basic innovation in the early years of development is likely to be an increase in the number of people who are exposed to formal schooling. This tends to shift functions from the family and church to a growing educational complex. The question, for those with some control over this trend in the beginning phases of development, is how rapid the extension of formal education should be and which level should receive emphasis.

The answer to this question requires a balancing of strictly economic considerations (such as the need for various skills,

---

[26] Neil J. Smelser, *The Sociology of Economic Life* (Englewood Cliffs, N.J.: Prentice-Hall, 1963), pp. 113–114.

specific and general, in the industrial and commercial sectors) with wider social considerations. Manpower issues must be related to sociological problems such as assuring a social milieu that will support development efforts. These needs may or may not be complementary, and educational policy in developing countries must take more than manpower problems (in the narrowest economic sense) into account.

Efforts to accelerate basic literacy by simply imposing elementary schools on a sector of society that has not yet begun to change, and where there is but slight ferment, has often borne little fruit in underdeveloped societies. George Foster has analyzed some of the problems:

> Usually the desire to read and write comes late in the development of peasant society. Villagers do not look upon literacy as an abstract thing that is good *per se*. It is something that takes time and hard work, and when it is achieved it has no meaning for most people. Berreman tells how, in a Himalayan foothill village, attitudes toward government school programs generally are not favorable. This attitude is due in considerable measure to the apparent absence of tangible benefits accruing to those people who have been educated in the past.[27]

Once a minimal social base on which to begin building universal elementary education is available, the school can be an accelerating factor in the development process. This implies enough portents of change in the society to create at least a latent concern about literacy among the masses. Some advantages of education must become evident to at least a certain number of people in the rural areas. (It should be remembered that rural people generally number about 60 to 80 per cent of the population in underdeveloped countries.)

Population and Education

Many of the underdeveloped countries face obstacles to development that are perhaps more difficult to surmount than those that were faced by today's developed countries. For one thing,

---

[27] George M. Foster, *Traditional Cultures and the Impact of Technological Change* (New York: Harper, 1962), p. 167.

many of these countries have huge populations that are rapidly growing larger. The developed nations of today had relatively small populations in their predevelopment stages. England, in 1750, had about eight million people; the United States, in the 1840's, numbered less than twenty million; Japan, in 1860, had a population of about thirty million; Germany, in the 1860's, had less than thirty million; other European countries such as Norway, Finland, the Netherlands, Sweden, Belgium, Switzerland, and Denmark had fewer than three million people in the beginning phases of development. This contrasts sharply with many underdeveloped countries today. For example, India has nearly 500 million people; China numbers about 750 million; Pakistan, 100 million; Indonesia, 100 million; Brazil, 80 million; Egypt, 30 million; Mexico, 40 million; Nigeria, 40 million; South Korea, 30 million. As Kuznets points out:

> It is often overlooked, although not by demographers, that the large populations of the developed countries today are a consequence, not an antecedent of their rapid economic growth; and that at the crucial earlier stages the population groups were small .... This difference in sheer population size between the developed countries in their preindustrial phase and at least some of the larger underdeveloped countries today should be added to the others [problems] of development already noted.[28]

Not only are many of the backward countries already densely populated, but their rates of growth in numbers are greater than those of the older developed countries in their predevelopment phase. Also, the developed countries could take advantage of the escape valve provided by the existence of relatively empty lands willing to take large numbers of migrants. During the nineteenth century, Europe had a net emigration of some fifty million people to the Western hemisphere alone. No such massive migration is possible today since the formerly empty countries now are quite well populated and have policies that limit immigration to relatively small numbers.

These demographic facts may imply that educational advance

[28] Simon Kuznets, "Underdeveloped Countries and the Pre-Industrial Phase in the Advanced Countries" in A. N. Agarwala and S. P. Singh, eds., *The Economics of Underdevelopment* (New York: Oxford University Press, 1963), p. 147.

more rapid than that which occurred in the now-developed countries could be of key importance. It appears that under certain
circumstances educational gains are likely to depress fertility.
This seems to be the case particularly in countries that are already
somewhat urbanized, with a fairly large proportion of the population literate, and a relatively high median (say six to seven years)
of school years completed. However, educational efforts aimed
directly at a decrease in fertility may also have important effects
in less developed areas.

One effort to clarify the gains to be made by diverting some
resources that might have been used for physical investment, or
for general educational expansion, to a program of adult education aimed directly at reducing fertility is found in a paper by
John Isbister on the situation in Korea.[29] Noting that a major
educational effort to reduce fertility is now under way in that
country, Isbister has calculated the population growth in Korea
that may be expected if the program succeeds, and on the other
hand, the population to be expected if present fertility and mortality rates persist over the period from 1960 to 1990. He also
makes projections of the total national product that might be
expected in 1990 under each assumption. Because the reduction
in fertility due to the large-scale education program of family
planning would reduce the dependency ratio markedly by the late
1970's and 1980's, there could be more saving and investment in
those years. With lowered fertility, the dependency ratio in Korea
would be 1.3 dependents to each worker by 1990, while continued
high fertility would not allow any change by 1990 in the 1960
dependency ratio of 1.8.

Furthermore, since additional workers in the Korean context
add little or nothing to the volume of production, a smaller work
force would not, in itself, significantly reduce the total product
created over the period. Thus, because of greater capital available
per worker and the low or zero marginal productivity of labor, it
is estimated that total national product under the reduced fertility
projection would grow (in constant dollars) from $1.6 billion in

[29] John Isbister, "Family Planning and Economic Growth in Developing Countries," *Background Papers*, International Conference on Family Planning Programs (Geneva, Switzerland: August 23–27, 1965), pp. 4–19.

1960 to $7.8 billion; with continued high fertility it is estimated that total product would grow from $1.6 billion to only $7.0 billion. Since, with the successful fertility reduction campaign, there would be a larger total product in 1990 and fewer people to whom it would be distributed, the per person income would be $169 in 1990. With constant fertility, the per person income in 1990 would be $111.

Ceylon, Korea, Taiwan, Singapore, Chile, and Puerto Rico are examples of areas where investment in adult education programs of birth control is likely to produce higher per capita income in the long run than any other form of similar cost investment, whether in physical capital or in other forms of education. Hopefully, Pakistan, India, Egypt, Indonesia, and other countries at similar levels are approaching a level of development that will accept investment in family limitation education as a practical measure. Most of Africa and parts of Latin America (including Haiti, Bolivia, Guatemala, and others) may not be appropriate places for such investment until many decades from now.

Thus, it appears that governments in high-fertility countries may want to put more into education than would be indicated by manpower projections alone. This would be especially relevant if such an allocation did one of two things: (*a*) increase the level of education to the point where education, in itself, would tend to bring down fertility, or (*b*) increase the level of education to the point where a specific additional educational effort, oriented directly toward the small family ideal and the understanding of fertility control, would have a good prospect of success.

It would seem, in countries too depressed in basic educational achievements, that adult education in fertility control has little effect, and the results of this type of program may not justify the cost. J. M. Stycos found that Haiti was just such an area.

> When one's general lot in life is determined by vague forces extraneous to the individual, and when numbers of children are viewed in the same context, there is simply no solid foundation on which to build a program of family limitation. The only hope lies in raising education levels ... to a certain minimum point at which self-improvement seems both possible and desirable. Indeed it is precisely at this point that general programs are most needed and make most sense. At one end of the continuum, population con-

trol programs are impracticable, at the other end largely unnecessary.[30]

Educational programs aimed at fertility control will probably be most successful in areas of high fertility, where literacy rates exceed 50 per cent and school enrollment ratios of those between 5 and 19 years of age approach or have passed 50 per cent.

The gains in per capita income due to successful fertility control education programs can theoretically be forecast and should be taken into account when considering educational priorities. The problem is more complicated than merely projecting manpower or other needs, while leaving growth of population as a given constant.

Education and the Economy

It has become popular to apply certain economic categories to education. Education is called an "investment" that has a certain economic "return." Measurements of educational "capital" and differential "pay-offs" of education have been calculated, particularly in the United States. The implication is that education can be fitted in with traditional economic variables and that judgments about its relative economic merits can be made *vis-à-vis* other uses of resources.

The difficulties in attempting to see the relationship of education to the economy in this way are (1) the improbability of adequately measuring the external economies of education, those benefits that accrue to others because of the increasing education gained by those being educated; (2) the fact that the superior income of the educated person, especially in underdeveloped countries, may be, and often is, due to traditional class and caste influences or to monopolistic controls which the better-educated classes may have in various fields of production; and (3) the possibility that the economic advantage of the educated portion of the population is due to an intrinsic superiority to which education, in itself, bears little relation.

In spite of the difficulties encountered in the most exact and

[30] J. Mayone Stycos, "Experiments in Social Change: The Caribbean Fertility Studies," in Clyde V. Kiser, ed., *Research in Family Planning* (Princeton: Princeton University Press, 1963), p. 147.

rigorous efforts to calculate the contribution of education, some insight can be gained into its economic value. For example, studies of the American economy over a number of years show that total output, measured as gross national product (GNP), has increased at a higher rate than the rate of increase of the two inputs, capital and labor. Bowen has argued that the size of this discrepancy (called the residual) is so large in the American data that more exploration of the economic effects of such factors as education is certainly indicated. "It seems clear that the simple accumulation of physical capital, in and of itself, has not played the dominant role in economic growth sometimes ascribed to it."[31]

The qualitative issue is sometimes overlooked when the economic gains from education are considered. Especially in underdeveloped countries, the quality and spirit of the education is of great significance in any assessment of education and economic growth. Even though education may increase in amount, it may be of the wrong kind. "An unemployable, but educated class can be the cause of uncertainty and risk prejudicial to economic activity, and young people brought up to despise manual work can reinforce the resistances to development."[32]

Obviously, education has a "consumption" side as well as an "investment" component. If education is viewed and used only as a means of entry into an outmoded elite, or purely as an aesthetic experience in humanistic study, it is not likely to increase the economic contribution of the recipient very much. The "consumption" aspect of education unfortunately is relatively more prevalent in the underdeveloped world, where it can be afforded least, than in the advanced countries, where consumption aspects of education can be borne more easily.

Education and the Polity

Although a few nations have progressed in spite of cultural schisms, or diversity in language or religion, a certain amount of

[31] William G. Bowen, *Economic Aspects of Education* (Princeton: Princeton University, Industrial Relations Section, 1964), p. 316.

[32] Thomas Balogh, "The Economics of Educational Planning: Sense and Nonsense," *Comparative Education Review*, Vol. 1, No. 1 (October 1964), p. 9.

political unity is necessary to support development. Americans are fond of pointing to their pluralistic nation, but, in fact, a remarkable similarity of outlook, language, and behavior exists in the United States. In underdeveloped countries, the cultural, linguistic, and religious splits are often very serious and are certainly debilitating to development efforts. A proper development effort demands a stable polity, which in turn must have broad loyalty from nearly all sections of the society.

The problems of maintaining a stable polity in the face of large diversities is well exemplified in the case of India. Humayin Kabir, an Indian educator, recently wrote that "the growing generations must be trained to be Indians who accept their total heritage."[33] He felt that since elementary-school courses in history are, by their very nature, highly selective, the material chosen should not emphasize sectional loyalties and concerns. The things that India, as India, has accomplished should be the focus. This does not demand distortion of history, but it does mean a conscious effort to write texts and teach in a way that emphasizes unity more than diversity. What is true for history also applies to literature and other humanistic and social courses of study. Kabir argues that every effort should be made to establish interstate cultural exchange in India. "Such programmes should be further expanded, so that people in one area or cultural tradition in India may become familiar with the culture of other areas or traditions and recognize elements of similarity which will strengthen the sense of national solidarity."[34]

Education has been given credit in some of the developed countries for reducing serious diversity. The Americanization of the children of immigrants to the United States, the creation of a German nationalism in the various petty states during the first half of the nineteenth century, and the increasing acceptance recently of Yugoslav nationalism as opposed to Croatian, Serbian, Macedonian, and Slovenian loyalties are all examples of the use of education to reduce the stronger types of diversity.

If steps in education are successfully taken to increase the

[33] Humayin Kabir, "Education and National Integration in India," in John W. Hanson and Cole S. Brembeck, eds., *Education and the Development of Nations* (New York: Holt, Rinehart and Winston, 1966), p. 244.
[34] *Ibid.*, p. 246.

attachment of the people to the national state, governments in their turn will be forced to accelerate actions to advance the process of development. This may be especially important, for many existing governments are controlled by landed and conservative commerical interests which, as Baron points out, cannot be expected to readily "design and execute a set of measures running counter to each and all of their immediate vested interests."[35] Further, this alliance will not "abdicate" of its own volition, nor does it change in response to incantation.[36] But if education can create greater attachment to the national state symbol, it will be less easy for reactionary governments to sustain power by using "divide and rule" tactics. Ironically, a greater attachment to the national state may mean deposing the agents of that state in many underdeveloped countries. Paradoxically, some reactionary governments are supporting education programs which, if successful, are likely to create greater pressure for government reform, if not revolution.

Summary

It seems fairly evident that the educational systems of the developed countries are among the most crucial underlying supports for the continuing existence of these nations as developed societies. Without widespread literacy, technological competence, and national cohesion, the whole fabric of developed society would begin to unravel.

The exact role that education played in bringing about the past transformation of the societies now developed is a matter of some debate. But that educational changes were tied in to the final maturation of these societies is not to be doubted. The role of education has seemed more clear-cut in countries like Japan or Russia, which have matured later, than in the case of England, the earliest country to develop. Also, the crucial level at which formal education either in quantitative or qualitative terms has entered into the development process has surely varied from country to country.

[35] Paul A. Baron, "The Political Economy of Backwardness," in Agarwala and Singh, *op. cit.,* p. 88.
[36] *Ibid.,* p. 90.

The expectation that education can be of singular significance in bringing about progress in the populations of the underdeveloped world may be well founded, but it must be remembered that demographic conditions are often more unfavorable than they were in the case of the now developed world. Also, narrow efforts to see educational processes in a simple economic manpower context may overlook wider sociological and qualitative questions which, although difficult to make precise, must not be neglected. Finally, the conservatism of political power arrangements must not be treated lightly and may frustrate the most elaborate visions of those dedicated to education and development.

Suggested Readings for Chapter II

ADAMS, DONALD K., and ROBERT BJORK. "Modernization as Affected by Governmental and International Educational Influences: Japan," in Stewart Fraser, ed., *Governmental Policy and International Education*. New York: Wiley, 1965.

ANDERSON, C. ARNOLD, AND MARY JEAN BOWMAN, eds. *Education and Economic Development*. Chicago: Aldine, 1965.

BALOGH, THOMAS. "The Economics of Educational Planning: Sense and Nonsense." *Comparative Education Review*, Vol. I, No. 1 (October 1964).

BOWEN, WILLIAM G. *Economic Aspects of Education*. Princeton: Princeton University, Industrial Relations Section, 1964.

BURNS, HOBERT, ed. *Education and the Development of Nations*. Syracuse: Syracuse University Press, 1963.

CURLE, ADAM. "Education, Politics, and Development." *Comparative Education Review*, Vol. VII, No. 3 (1964).

HANSON, JOHN W., and COLE S. BREMBECK, eds. *Education and the Development of Nations*. New York: Holt, Rinehart and Winston, 1966.

HARBISON, FREDERICK H., and CHARLES A. MYERS. *Education, Manpower, and Economic Growth*. New York: McGraw-Hill, 1964.

McCLELLAND, DAVID C. "Does Education Accelerate Economic Growth?" *Economic Development and Cultural Change*, Vol. 14, No. 3 (April 1966), pp. 257–278.

SCHULTZ, THEODORE W. *The Economic Value of Education*. New York: Columbia University Press, 1963.

VAIZEY, JOHN. *The Economics of Education*. London: Faber and Faber, 1962.

CHAPTER III

Patterns of Educational Poverty: Middle Africa

When, in Chapter II, we defined the development process and the role that education may have in it, no great emphasis was put on the social and physical variations that exist among poor nations. Some societies, in the length of their period of nationhood, are old, some new. Some have rich natural resources, some few. Some have a long history of advanced development in certain cultural areas; some are only now being exposed to the attributes of advanced civilization.

Serious attention must be given to these variations in any descriptive account of regional educational development. This chapter and the two following will focus on patterns of educational poverty as exhibited in three geocultural areas of the underdeveloped world: Middle Africa, South Asia, and Latin America. In examining intraregional and interregional differences, attention will be given to both quantitative and qualitative social and educational characteristics selected to illustrate the nature of the problem of development in these areas.

Our analysis will concentrate on the formal educational process, with particular attention to educational policies and programs within the social context. Linkages between the educational efforts and such broad national goals as social justice and economic growth will be examined. In so doing we will try to be sensitive to the influences of residue colonialism, dominant cultural values, and the expressed social and economic goals, as these impinge on the functions of schools and universities. Therefore, while some information concerning organization, curriculum, and teaching methods may be included, no attempt will be made to provide comprehensive descriptions of the educational systems being analyzed.

Of the geocultural areas under consideration, Middle Africa (the huge amorphous region stretching from the Sahara Desert in the north to the Republic of South Africa in the south) generally has had the shortest history of experiencing the demonstration effects of development. Although geographically closer to Europe (the first developed area) than most underdeveloped regions, until the twentieth century Middle Africa's intercourse with Europe was sporadic and on a relatively small scale, as compared, for example, with the eighteenth- and nineteenth-century intercourse between South Asia or Latin American and Europe. Moreover, although there is some evidence that rather remarkable cultures flourished in Africa some 800 to 1,000 years ago and that powerful empires were built in western Africa during the fourteenth to sixteenth centuries, contemporary Africa cannot boast a level of natural-resource development or formal educational heritage equivalent to those of Asia and Latin America.

While contacts with Europe were not great until this century, every contemporary African culture has felt the impact of contact with European peoples and institutions. Sea traders, Christian proselytizers, waves of European colonists, and recently cadres of technical assistance workers, scholars, and entrepreneurs from the developed nations have all combined to influence African social institutions. Particularly since World War II, African students and government officials in increasingly large numbers have begun participating in extended and intensive firsthand experiences in Western nations.

Yet elements for continuity as well as for change are still highly visible in Africa. Traditional institutions in the form of the extended family, animistic and ancestral religions, ascriptive authority arrangements, and particularistic legal codes still exist. Nor has the legacy of long periods of colonialism (affecting all of Middle Africa except Liberia and Ethiopia) been entirely a modernizing influence. Colonial policies and institutions at times assumed a rigidity which thwarted the necessary adaptation to the African scene.

In describing education in Middle Africa, a brief look will first be given to colonial policies, particularly those related to education. Second, an attempt will be made to summarize the extent of educational variation (in terms of level of development) that has existed among Middle African nations. Last, the focus will be placed on the contemporary educational scene, examining its quantitative and qualitative development.

Colonial Educational Policies

France, Great Britain, and Belgium emerged as the major victors from the contest for control of Middle Africa. Although the policies of these colonial powers reflected their own political, social, and economic attitudes, certain broad similarities are discernible. First, the original purpose of colonization was to provide economic gain to the European power. The African was of little concern except as a means toward that end, but his usefulness seemed to increase as he gained at least some education, and Africans with a certain amount of Western schooling assumed positions as clerks and lower-echelon civil servants. Second, the people who were most concerned and involved with the African personality and society were missionaries. Regardless of the educational policies of the colonial power, much of the actual schooling in Africa was provided by missionary groups, even though they were subsidized after World War I and regulated to a greater or lesser degree by the government. The missionary groups typically viewed education as an auxiliary to their primary goal of Christianizing Africa. They believed that an African who could read and write either his own language or a European one and was familiar with some facets of Western culture would be a more likely convert and later a more stable Christian. Therefore, they concentrated their teaching and resources on providing primary education for as many as possible. Missions also controlled the majority of the secondary schools in preindependence Africa, but efforts at this level typically were not seen as their main thrust.

British Policy

British colonial policy was theoretically based on "indirect rule," which meant that the policies of the government would be administered to as great a degree as possible through the existing indigenous institutions. Furthermore, "the traditional leaders of African societies were to be gradually taught to assume more enlightened responsibilities and their institutions were to change slowly toward more advanced forms."[1] The extent of indirect rule varied, however, according to the Africans' level of development, their form of government, and the number of white settlers.

As a part of indirect rule there evolved the doctrine of "differentiation" on which educational policy was based. This meant, in principle, the creation of separate insitutions appropriate to African, rather than to European, needs. In the schools, for example, instruction was given in the vernacular at the early primary levels, and more extensive or special schooling was provided for future chiefs. In areas where Asian, European, and African populations existed, three separate school systems were maintained. Educational policies on the part of British administrations, however, were not regularized or focused, due to the practice of colonial self-support. Therefore, the amount and type of education were largely determined by the initiative of local colonial officers and the willingness of the colonial population to support the schools financially.

The attempt to educate the African within his environment was undermined in the British colonies, however, by the use of British External examinations. These were administered in London or in the colonies, and the studies that were undertaken to pass them were, by necessity, non-African. Furthermore, the economic advantages, as well as the prestige derived from passing these tests, led Africans to demand the Europeanized curriculum and, in some instances, to regard African-oriented education as a European attempt to keep them in subjugation.

French Policy

The doctrine of "assimilation" provided the stated guidelines for French colonial policy. Its purpose was "to integrate the overseas possessions with France, to assimilate the colonial

---

[1] Francis K. Sutton, "Education and the Making of Modern Nations," in James S. Coleman, ed., *Education and Political Development* (Princeton: Princeton University Press, 1965), p. 64.

people into the body of French political, social and cultural thought and practice."[2] Ignoring indigenous institutions, the French established a highly centralized administration modeled on that of France. In accordance with the principles of assimilation, yet also in recognition of the vast numbers of tribesmen to be assimilated, the idea of "association" was developed as the basis for educational policies. Association meant that a small, elite group of Africans would be educated to occupy a leadership role and would be granted the full rights and privileges of French citizenship.[3] The elite were chosen on the basis of their academic ability, although future chiefs generally were included, no matter what their talents. There was one system of schools, open to all ethnic groups, in which French was the language of instruction from the earliest grades, and the curricula and textbooks were patterned after those of France.

Nevertheless, French education in Africa was different in many ways from education in France. In the first place, the French, like the British, followed a policy of colonial self-support which meant that the extent of schooling provided varied greatly from area to area. Second, for the elite only, those courses were offered that would train students for positions in which a particular need existed. Third, the diplomas awarded, although on a par with those of France, were always identified as colonial and therefore were not of the same economic or social value.[4] Finally, great emphasis was placed on the primary school as an institution of terminal vocational education, and access to any higher levels was extremely limited, even more so than in France.

French colonial policy changed considerably after World War II. France sought to create a union of Franch states, with the African areas classified as overseas territories. This policy brought with it the granting of full French citizenship to all

[2] Quoted in T. Walter Wallbank's *Contemporary Africa: Continent in Transition* (Princeton: Van Nostrand, 1956), p. 42.
[3] However, it has been noted that "the few instances in which French citizenship was granted were exceptional and did not result from a systematic policy." Michel Debeauvois, "Education in Former French Africa," in Coleman, *op. cit.*, p. 80.
[4] *Ibid.*

Africans living in French territory and greatly increased emphasis
on aid and development.

The economic importance of education was made clear in the
*Educational Report of the Committee for Modernization of the
Overseas Territories,* published in 1948. The report was concerned with all of France's overseas territories (with the exception
of those in North Africa and Indochina), and while the recommendations were phrased in general terms, the overall goal was to
link educational change with the economic development of the
territories. Emphasis in the report was placed on the need for
careful planning and avoidance of the dangers of haphazard
educational development.

> Education should be adapted to the economic activity of each
> territory. Thus, technical education should concentrate solely on
> agriculture in French Equatorial Africa ... on polyvalent subjects
> in French West Africa and Madagascar. The level of such educa-
> tion should naturally vary according to the degree of evolution in
> each territory. In one, proficient farmers and skilled workers could
> be trained; in another, measures could be taken to train specialized
> technicians, doctors, or engineers.[5]

While the French initiated rapid expansion at all levels of education in their African colonies, vocational and agricultural
education were particularly emphasized. During this process of
educational growth, the French government established support
through direct financial grants, by increasing scholarships for
African students to study in France, and by recruiting French
teachers to send to the colonies.

Belgian Policy

Belgian policy, as illustrated in the Belgian Congo (now the
Democratic Republic of the Congo—Leopoldville), assumed a
long period of colonial relationship between the parent nation
and the colony. Unlike the British, for example, the Belgians
allowed little African participation in political bodies at any
level. First consideration was given to the attainment of a mini-

[5] L. Gray Cowan, James O'Connell, and David G. Scanlon, eds., *Education and
Nation-Building in Africa* (New York: Praeger, 1965), p. 74.

mum standard of material welfare through the development of productive skills. Consequently, educational emphasis was on literacy and rudimentary vocational training.

Statements on education from Belgian authorities consistently stressed the need to tailor schooling to the African environment and to make it "practical." Because of this bias, and for obvious economic reasons, the educational emphasis was on primary education. A few years of schooling would suffice to produce an efficient work force to exploit the great mineral deposits of the Congo area. One observer suggests that Belgian policy was based on the following assumption:

> It is better to have 90 per cent of the population capable of understanding what the government is trying to do for them and competent to help the government in doing it than to have 10 per cent of the population so full of learning that it spends its time telling the government what to do.[6]

To an even greater degree than the British and French, the Belgians relied almost exclusively on missionaries to run the schools. Not until well after World War II was any sizable number of schools opened under lay personnel. Enrollments in grades beyond the primary level remained very limited, and the first institution of higher education was not founded until 1954.

Intraregional Forces for Continuity and Change in Education

Several attempts have been made at subdividing Middle Africa in order to show the range of variation. Criteria such as religion, colonial or former colonial status, type of political system, and mode of livelihood have been used. For example, a noted anthropologist, Melville Herskovits, classifies the traditional cultures of Middle Africa into (1) pastoral societies (which predominate in East and Central Africa) and (2) agriculturally based societies (mainly in West Africa and the Congo Basin).[7] Another classification of "culture areas," advanced by the Ottenbergs,

[6]George H. T. Kimble, *Tropical Africa* (New York: Twentieth Century Fund, 1960), II, 115.
[7]Melville J. Herskovits, "Peoples and Cultures of Sub-Saharan African," *Annals,* No. 298 (March 1955), pp. 15–19.

suggests that three major areas may be found in Middle Africa: (1) the Central African, characterized by heavy rainfall and predominantly inhabited by agricultural peoples; (2) the Guinea Coast, also primarily agricultural (although some fishing exists); and (3) the East African Highlands and the Ethiopian Highlands, where both pastoral ·and agricultural forms of productivity are found but where cattle are of importance throughout.[8] These distinctions are helpful but not fully satisfactory in examining social and economic differences found in the region. To get the full flavor of the intraregional variations, particularly as these impinge on development and education, other factors must be considered.

The Effect of Colonization by Europeans

Europeans settled where profit was to be made, and preferably in the areas of more comfortable climate. Essentially, this meant the coastal cities of West Africa, the highlands of East Africa, and around the mineral deposits of Central Africa. Wherever large numbers of European colonists settled, a white aristocracy developed that limited the political activity and social mobility of the African.[9] Race friction resulting from European attitudes of superiority and lack of respect for the Africans were common in the "settler" countries. Moreover, where large numbers of whites settled as in the highlands of East Africa, two separate societies and economies developed. Until recently most Africans in these areas were part of a subsistence economy, and the few who became involved in the market economy had their occupational choices largely limited to the more menial jobs. Separate school systems, segregated by race, were maintained.

Yet the presence of Europeans provided stimulation for development. They needed a labor supply for their farms and mines which required temporary migration of African men away from their villages. Wage work weakened village life and partly "de-

[8] Simon and Phoebe Ottenberg, eds., *Cultures and Societies of Africa* (New York: Random House, 1960), pp. 8–10.

[9] In West Africa, where there were fewer European settlers, Africans served in legislative councils in the 1920's. In East Africa, however, it was not until World War II that Africans were nominated to legislative bodies.

tribalized" the men, thus stimulating change. The trading centers established by Europeans at such West African cities as Lagos, Freetown, and Accra became some of the most developed urban areas and thus acted as loci for further modernization.

However, European influence spread out not only from the little islands of economic activity but also from mission stations and schools. The extent of educational opportunity for the African, until recently, correlated closely with the intensity of mission activity. Most of the contemporary African leaders were educated at least in part by mission schools. These tribal groups, such as the Tonga of Malawi, whose geographical accessibility made them the first targets of mission education, were able to gain a disproportionate number of the more attractive government jobs open to Africans.

The Effects of Language Diversity

Most of the more than eight hundred languages spoken on the African continent can be found somewhere in Middle Africa. Some of these—the Kutuba of the Congo (Brazzaville), Twi, Ga, and others of Ghana—are purely local and serve only a fraction of the population even in the nations where they are official. Other languages such as Hausa, in Nigeria and other parts of West Africa, and Swahili (as well as Arabic) in East Africa, are well developed and widely spoken.

An indication of the severity of the language diversity problems can be seen in the Sudan where more than one hundred local languages exist. Many of these are spoken by only a few thousand people, and only five or six are spoken by more than 100,000. A dozen, perhaps, appear in written forms; but their "literature" consists almost exclusively of Bible translations. In one regard, however, the Sudan must consider itself relatively well off, for Arabic is spoken by approximately two-thirds of the population.

Most of the African languages, with the exception of Swahili, which was originally written in the Arabic script and has a considerable literature, remained unwritten until the arrival of Christian missionaries. The emphasis placed by some colonial governments and missions on education in the vernacular language gave

impetus to the further development of literature in those languages. Much, however, remains to be done in technically refin-
ing the indigenous languages and producing a supply of printed
materials appropriate for the increasing number of tropical Africans who are literate only in a local tongue.

The multiplicity of languages obviously places a burden on the
schools. The extent of the learning problems imposed, the retard-
ation in academic achievement, and the limitations in concep-
tualization remain largely unresearched. Clear, however, are the
successes of the schools in acting as the medium for the development of a common national language. A common language, in
turn, has made possible effective communication among various
language groups and mobilization of large numbers of citizens in
the joint effort of nation building.

The Effects of Rural Predominance and Recent Urbanization

Except in Nigeria, there were no sizable urban areas in pre-
European Middle Africa. It follows, of course, that where cities
developed, European settlers exercised complete political and economic control over them. Although the level of urbanization is
still not high in Middle Africa, urban growth presents both problems and possibilities in the course of development. To a large extent, except in terms of limits of residence imposed by Europeans
on Africans in some cities, the migration of rural Africans (pre-
ponderantly male until recently) to urban areas has been unplanned and uncontrolled.

Towns and cities are indices of development. Since the degree
of rurality is high in Middle Africa, and the social distance between rural and urban areas is generally greater than in most
underdeveloped regions, the process of urbanization has become
unusually important in producing change and development. Often the mobile, rural African may look to the town or city as a
source of temporary employment to fill an immediate material
need. In this manner, a class of peripatetic, semi-rural, semi-
urban Africans is being formed that provides extensive interaction
between city and village, with strong implications for change in
the latter. At subsequent stages of development the urban population will no doubt become more permanent.

The new urban areas are important as arenas for detribalization and acculturation of development patterns. In the town and
city the person's status is more likely to be achieved through
competence than ascribed through lineage. The growth of urban
social classes[10] and new associations with educational, trade-
union, religious, and political groups weaken tribal ties that have
been carried into the urban environment. Although disruptive
and destructive to traditional ways of life, African urban life can
provide security for some through salaried jobs and possibly a
sense of belonging, through new social and occupational groupings. As has been demonstrated by events in many of the post-
independent African nations, social groupings, commercial enterprises, and political power are by no means yet entirely divorced
from tribal attachments. To many Africans, urban substitutes
prove inadequate, and security is still to be found only in the
land.

Two crucial educational problems are inherent in the early
stages of urbanization in Middle Africa. First, urban educational
opportunity far exceeds that found in the rural areas. In Tanzania, for example, although only one rural child in four completing primary education in 1963 entered secondary school, one out
of two urban children were able to get into secondary school. In
Ghana, within urban areas, 55.4 per cent of all children of school-
going age were enrolled in school in 1960, as compared to 35.2
per cent in the rural areas.

A second problem concerns the drift of young people from
rural areas to cities. These persons usually have attended and
possibly completed primary schools and seek escape from rural
life and farming. Thus far in African development, unemployment from this source has been cumulative because the number
of young people leaving school has continually exceeded the employment opportunities.

There are no easy solutions to either of these problems. A

[10]As a gross generalization, class structure in urban Africa may be seen as a
three-layer affair. The upper stratum (excluding Europeans) might be called a
middle class, composed as it is of civil servants, a small professional group, and
white-collar workers. The next lower class is made up of skilled laborers, and
at the bottom is the laboring class. See Daniel McCall, "Dynamics of Urbanization in Africa," in Ottenberg and Ottenberg, *op. cit.,* pp. 522–533.

better diffusion of school facilities, and attention to cost and other factors that inhibit school attendance may help equalize educational opportunities. Creating a better fit between schooling and employment needs could also, of course, be brought about through reduction of school enrollments or through curtailing population increases. More immediately practical are schemes to create more jobs by speeding economic development, and creating and diffusing small industrial and commercial enterprises. "Ruralfication" and community development, by making local village life more attractive and rewarding, may serve to lessen the severity of both problems.

Cultural Variations in Receptivity to Change

Regardless of the degree of urbanization, language diversity, or relationship with Europe and Europeans, there are great differences in the basic value structures of many groups in Africa. Important variations exist in the manner of livelihood and the associated pattern of living. The Nilotic "cattle peoples" of East Africa, for example, value their herds not only as their chief means of subsistence but also as necessary components of their social and religious customs. Since cattle frequently are given as bride-price, the very continuance of the family line is dependent on their availability. Thus, any reform measures that would result in a reduction of the herds or lessen the possibilities of cattle ownership are looked upon with extreme disfavor.

In general, Nilotic pastoral tribes seem to oppose European innovations most strongly. One study suggests that the Pakot of Western Kenya "have maintained marked resistance to European innovations which have been attempted on political, religious, and economic fronts. Their resistance to change typified Nilotic people as a whole."[11] Pakot arguments against schooling are a case in point: "First, small boys assist in herding small stock, and putting them in school makes this impossible. Second, they see no value in learning reading, writing, or arithmetic; they do not envy European ways and have no desire to emulate them."[12]

[11] William R. Bascom and Melville J. Herskovits, eds., *Continuity and Change in African Cultures* (Chicago: University of Chicago Press, 1959), p. 159.
[12] *Ibid.*

The Pakot's resistance to outside influences appears to be based upon a "satisfaction with traditional culture and feeling that it is superior and more desirable than Euro-American civilization. This attitude, coupled with indifference or even contempt for other people, is shared by many Nilotic peoples who occupy portions of Sudan, Uganda and Kenya."[13]

In contrast with the Pakot, Masai, and other Nilotic peoples, the Chagga and Kikuyu of East Africa have been eager to adopt European ways.

Parallel intranation variations can be found in West Africa. Although there are several groups that resist change, extremely progressive ones can also be found. The highly individualistic Ibo of Nigeria, for example, are generally considered the group most receptive to change. The Ibo place strong emphasis on the ability to make one's own way in the world. The son of a prominent politician, for example, may have a head start on other men in his community, but he must validate this by his own abilities. Not only do personal qualities carry almost as much weight as seniority in secular leadership, but increasingly in contemporary times money has become the key to prestige.

Ibo society is characteristically "open," providing virtually all individuals with the possibility of enhancing status and prestige. Education is seen by the Ibo as an avenue to white-collar jobs in government, with posts in the native authority system, and positions in administration. Ibo society thus produces many business, professional, and political leaders who, while anticolonial, are not generally antagonistic to Western culture.

Group achievement is also stressed in Ibo culture. Villages, families, and other social units are often competitive in terms of size, wealth, and influence. Individuals are conscious of the relative status of the groups with which they are associated. European culture has given traditional group rivalries new dimensions, and villages now compete to build the first or best schools, or to improve their markets. Many social groups strive to push some of their "sons" ahead in schooling and to obtain scholarships in competition with other groups. However, individuals who obtain schooling, wealth, or political influence are expected to use their

[13] Harold K. Schneider, "Pakot Resistance to Change," *ibid.*, pp. 144–165.

new social standing to benefit the groups with which they are associated.[14]

The variations in receptivity to change are dependent on the cultural history of various groups, the structure of tribal society, and other more subtle factors. Without attempting to examine these causes further, it is important to recognize that such variations have implications for much of the subsequent discussion of education—particularly for the analyses of diffusion of education and educational planning.

Education and the Achievement of National Goals

The overriding goals of contemporary African nations are national unity, economic growth, and social justice. These goals mean, on the one hand, a rejection of much of the colonial and noncolonial past and, on the other hand, the utilization of selected existing institutions as part of the foundations of new societies. The popular term "Africanization" expresses the new focus on localization of institutions and personnel. In a more profound (and less clear) way, the intellectuals, artists, and political leaders, through the definition of such terms as "Negritude" and "African personality," seek nothing less than a full cultural renaissance.

To achieve national unity, a national identity has to be created among people whose affiliations traditionally have not extended beyond the tribal group. The school is increasingly seen as one means for the dissemination of the ideas and symbols of nationhood. Economic growth is also seen as closely tied to the school's ability to implant new attitudes and skills. Finally, social justice to most national leaders (who are also for the most part modernist) means efforts to equalize opportunities among segments of the population; and the schools, in particular, through adjustments in fees and promotion policies, are seen as instruments toward that end.

In considering the connection between education and these

---

[14] Simon Ottenberg, "Ibo Receptivity to Change," in Bascom and Herskovits, *op. cit.*, pp. 130–143. Ibo achievement of leadership positions out of proportion to their numbers was one of the irritants leading to intertribal conflict with the resultant movement toward the separate Ibo state, Biafra.

goals, attention will be focused on (1) the expansion and the social, racial, and regional equalization of educational opportunity and (2) educational planning.

Diffusion of Education through Classes and Regions

The arguments for greater diffusion of education are made in terms of all the major national goals, but most effectively in terms of national unity and social justice. The appeal of claims for social justice, whether viewed as a component of African socialism or not, has meant that national political and educational leaders have supported popularistic demands for rapid expansion at all educational levels. Leaders, by providing schooling for those groups which by accident or design had previously received little or none, have capitalized on the role of the school in establishing linkages between local and national goals.

The argument, frequently heard in Africa today, that the colonial policies (especially where sizable groups of European settlers were found) discriminated against Africans warrants attention. Certainly income differentials, for example, between African and non-African groups are striking. The pattern observable in Table III–1 could be replicated for the same time

TABLE III–1

Distribution of Working Population and Money Income
in Nyasaland (Malawi), 1954 and 1960

Racial Segment of the Population	Numbers Involved 1954	Average Yearly Earnings 1954	Numbers Involved 1960	Average Yearly Earnings 1960
Europeans	3,000	922	4,000	1,185
Asian and "colored"	1,000	448	2,000	556
African (wages and salaries group)	134,000	34	183,000	51
African (rural)	2,336,000	11	2,627,000	11

Source: *Nyasaland: Development Plan 1962–1963* (Zomba: Government Printer, n.d.), p. 18. Earnings listed in British pounds.

period in several other African countries, with only slight differences in degree.

Three facts in particular may be noted from the table. First, a small number of non-Africans earned on the average of forty to eighty times what Africans earned. Second, the great majority of African people derived a living from rural income. Third, while the numbers involved in each category of work rose between 1954 and 1960, and while the average annual income of members of each minority group also rose, the average annual income of the African rural majority remained unchanged.

In education, the racial disparities are also highly visible. When, in 1964, the new government of Zambia was faced with the problem of integrating the African and Federal (catering largely to non-African population) systems of education, the gap between the two became dramatically evident (Table III-2).

Further evidence that Europeans and Asians fared better in terms of educational financial allocation prior to independence is illustrated by the fact that in Tanganyika in 1959–1960 only 2.6 million £ were allocated by the government for 9 million Africans while 430,000 £ were allocated for a population of 100,000 Europeans and Asians.[15]

Intranational variation in the diffusion of education is visible throughout Middle Africa; yet, the goals of African nationalism and social justice demand equality of opportunity. It is clear that the immediate and overriding goal of national integration may be confounded if regional disparities are too strongly related to racial and tribal groupings. However, it should be kept in mind that the difference in education levels between European settlers and Africans does not imply that the Africans did not profit educationally by the presence of Europeans. In addition to the demonstration effect provided, European establishments, such as mining operations, recognized that a minimal education would add to the African's productivity. Thus, at the time of independence, the Congo had one of the highest primary enrollment ratios in Middle Africa. Further, the coastal cities of West Africa, where the

[15]John Cameron, "Integration of Education in Tanganyika," *Comparative Education Review*, Vol. XI, No. 1 (February 1967), p. 45.

TABLE III–2

Comparison of Federal and African Systems of Education
in Northern Rhodesia (Zambia), *circa* 1962

Features	Federal Schools	African Schools
Race	Mainly European and Asian	African
Compulsory education	All children aged 7–15	6 years (in designated *urban* areas only); 4 years elsewhere, where schools were available
Enrollment ratios	Very high	Very low, particularly so for girls
Access to higher education	No restrictions between stages other than those of merit, determined by examinations	Bottlenecks in provision of places at all grade levels
Wastage	Little wastage; mobility high through the system	Extremely high rate of dropouts—higher for girls than for boys
Pupil–teacher ratio	1 to 29	1 to 51 (some teachers worked double sessions with smaller numbers in a group. 40 considered a "model" class)
Annual expenditure per pupil	£90 (primary + secy.) per pupil for 20,942 pupils	£12 per pupil for 334,050 pupils
Language of instruction	One language of instruction—English	Two, often three, languages of instruction, Early primary—mother tongue. Middle primary on—1 of 4 official vernaculars + English increasingly introduced

Source: Maureen Webster, *Federal and African Systems of Education in Northern Rhodesia* (Syracuse: Syracuse University, 62 pages, mimeo).

exigencies of urban life forced more contact between African and European culture, saw rapid African educational advancement.

The British policy of indirect rule, emphasizing insularity of regions, tended to aggravate disparities of educational diffusion. For example, by 1948, in Ghana (the Gold Coast), "the proportion of the population with six years of education or more stood at 5.8 per cent of the colony, 3.9 per cent in Ashanti, but only 0.21 per cent in the Northern Territories."[16]

Many African leaders and Western observers are sanguine in their faith that the post-independence educational systems will obliterate ethnic imbalance within national "elites." In time this faith may be realized as a tradition of secular education develops (with "universal" criteria for selection and "achievement" criteria for promotion). Yet the time required for an educational system to perform this function may be surprisingly long. The Ghanaian system, for example, is greater in size and maturity than that of the Ivory Coast; it has proportionately more secondary-school places, and these are more geographically diffused about the country. Nevertheless, the Ghanaian pupil with a certain ethnic background frequently is far less successful in getting into postprimary education than is the typical pupil in the Ivory Coast.[17] That is, although Ghana has made notable progress in the extension of educational opportunity, particularistic criteria still influence the nature of postprimary-school enrollment considerably.

Education has also affected intranational arrangements of political power. The tribal or culture groups most receptive, or having the easiest access to education, reaped rewards through the attainment of positions of political power. A side effect of this phenomenon has been a further impetus for political parties to arise around subnational, tribal, or other groups.[18]

[16]"Gold Coast, *Census of Population*, 1948" in Philip J. Foster, "Ethnicity and the Schools in Ghana," *Comparative Education Review*, Vol. VI, No. 2 (October 1962), p. 129.

[17]Remi Clignet and Philip Foster, "Potential Elites in Ghana and the Ivory Coast," *American Journal of Sociology*, Vol. 70 (November 1964), p. 357.

[18]Gabriel A. Almond and James S. Coleman, eds., *The Politics of the Developing Areas* (Princeton: Princeton University Press, 1960), pp. 281–282.

Education and the Modernization of African Values

The special role of Western education in fostering changes in the African social stratification should be noted. As one of the most important and apparent examples, schooling, when taken from the family by the churches and governments, served to weaken the kin group. Not only did the family lose control of education but education no longer served traditional patterns of socialization. Education through schools frequently meant formation of new loyalties and training for non-local occupations, thus creating new types of associations and altering the older pattern of stratification.

Under the colonial powers, education had meant access, for a few Africans, to prestigious clerical positions. This tradition, coupled, after independence, with a tendency toward extreme centralization of power in the national governments, has perpetuated strong aspirations for white-collar work. From the results of scattered inquiries it would appear that a great majority of students aspire to professional and white-collar employment. Since such positions are linked to higher pay, power, and prestige, such aspirations are entirely rational.

In addition to being the instrument for creating a clerkly class indispensable to colonial rule in the past, education also created the new modernist African political elite. As has been pointed out, educational policies among the colonial powers varied considerably. Where significant opportunities existed for higher education abroad, as they did for French and British West Africans, a prestigious and confident African political elite formed comparatively early. In those parts of Middle Africa where advanced education was nonexistent, or severely limited (as in the former Belgian areas, much of East Africa, and Ethiopia), a political elite (and mass political mobilization) was slow in developing.

Another aspect of the influence of education concerns its effect on the degree of social mobility. The case of Ghana is illustrative. By Middle African standards, Ghana exhibits a highly developed economy and educational system. Nevertheless, its occupational structure is typical of many African nations, and its rapid rate of educational expansion finds parallels throughout

Africa. In Ghana, the occupational structure is highly constricted at the summit, with only 6.9 per cent of adult males engaged in professional, higher technical, and administrative and clerical occupations (1960), as compared with 62.8 per cent in farming and fishing. In response to public demand and political leadership, primary- and secondary-school enrollments have increased dramatically (from 271,000 in 1950 to 1,200,000 in 1963). Certain significant characteristics of this upsurge are noticeable:

1. Employment opportunities in the modern sector of the economy have not kept pace with expansion in education.

2. Secondary education is increasingly becoming mandatory for positions once held by those with primary-school education. Primary schooling, therefore, is decreasingly a guarantee of upward mobility.

3. Increased opportunities for primary and middle schooling have been paralleled by relatively decreased opportunities for secondary schooling. (That is, the proportion of those admitted to secondary schools from the graduates of lower schools is smaller.)

4. Because of the importance of secondary education, Ghana is now faced with a growing demand for secondary places.[19]

Thus Ghana, unlike many nations in Africa, offers an example of an educational system that has produced more output than can be absorbed. The poor fit which exists between schooling and employment may well be experienced soon by other nations permitting extremely rapid educational growth at the primary and secondary levels. Although the Seven-Year Development Plan of Ghana envisages a level of economic growth that by 1970 will be capable of absorbing the total output of the educational system, this can prove to be the case only if certain modifications are made in the aspirations of the graduates of the primary and middle schools. That is, one implication of universal education is that eventually all jobs in a community must be carried out by persons who have had some education.[20]

Again, using Ghana for illustrative purposes, one finds that ac-

19 Foster, *op. cit.,* pp. 159–171.
20 Walter Birmingham, I. Neustadt, and E. N. Omaboe, *A Study of Contemporary Ghana* (Evanston: Northwestern University Press, 1967), II, 231–238.

cess to secondary schools is correlated with the urban background of students and parental socioeconomic status. Nevertheless, Foster concludes:

> Although the offspring of "white collar" workers obtain a disproportionate share of secondary school places it is equally important to note in the case of boys that over one-third are the children of rural farmers and fishermen, the overwhelming bulk of whom are totally illiterate. . . . It can only be concluded that these institutions are extraordinarily successful in drawing from a very wide segment of the Ghanaian population.[21]

If Foster's conclusions about Ghana are correct, and if the Ghana case has implications for the rest of Middle Africa, we may expect the African schools in the earlier stages of development to play a more significant role in the dissemination of symbols of modernization than they played in Western societies.

Traditionally, with the exception of privileged positions based on race, Africa has not exhibited well-defined social classes or distinctive class subcultures. This fact has led to patterns of secondary education presently less tied to social class than those of Europe, and the broad base of support for these systems, in turn, has inhibited the emergence of a social class-related schooling. Finally, the egalitarian foundations of schooling, plus the demands placed on schooling by development goals, may combine to promote a relatively rapid expansion of secondary and higher education. Yet, as the Ghana case suggests, while at present the educational system itself may not strongly reflect elitist interests, there are already some signs of class consciousness related to education. It is difficult to judge how far this will go as Africa develops in coming years.

Educational Planning

Although increasing attention was paid to education by the colonial governments in the postwar years, growth was slow, at least in relation to the size of the school-age population. Some

---

[21] Foster, *op. cit.*, p. 163. Foster further points out that this was not characteristic of nineteenth-century western Europe "when its occupational structure was not entirely dissimilar to that of contemporary Ghana and when secondary schooling was in comparable supply."

statistics for the years 1960–1963, at which time most Middle
African nations were independent or about to become so, will
give an idea of the impact of this lack of attention. At the primary level, most of these nations enrolled between 30 and 70 per
cent of the children in the eligible age group. This enrollment,
however, was largely concentrated in the first or second grades.
Even in Kenya—one of the educationally more favored East
African nations—high wastage rates in the upper grades are
noticeable. In 1965 the enrollments in Standards I and VII were
190,432 and 117,563, respectively.[22]

To further illustrate this point, the proportion of pupils completing the full primary course in Tanzania (1961) was 4 per cent
of those who entered, in Zambia 8 to 9 per cent (1964), and in
Malawi 25 per cent (1964). The retention rates generally were
somewhat better in the educationally more advanced West African nations, with Ghana's sixth-grade enrollment (1964) more
than one-fourth of the enrollment in grade one, and Nigeria's
fifth-grade enrollment (Western Region, 1964) over one-half of
that of grade one.

At the secondary level, only Ghana and Nigeria (Lagos) had
an enrollment ratio of above 10 per cent. In most countries fewer
than 3 per cent of secondary-school-age children were in school.
In none of these countries was as much as 1 per cent of the appropriate age group enrolled in higher education.

Low enrollments and high wastage rates were not the only
problems inherited by the newly-independent Middle African nations. Education of girls was significantly less advanced than that
of boys. Of the fewer than ten million children enrolled in both
primary and secondary schools in 1961, two-thirds were boys; and
at the secondary level, only one-fifth of the student population
was female. At the higher level, in addition to low female enrollments, there was a disproportionate emphasis on liberal arts,
with few students of either sex pursuing courses in scientific or
technological fields, or involved in African studies.

High wastage rates, gross differences in educational opportunities between sexes, disparities regarding educational availability

[22]James R. Sheffield, ed., *Education, Employment and Rural Development*
(Nairobi: East African Publishing House, 1967), p. 369.

in rural and urban areas, an alarming rate of unemployment among primary-school leavers,[23] the demands of expanding economies, and the need to conserve scarce resources all have contributed to a growing awareness in Africa of the merits of educational planning. The first important efforts in this direction were two regional conferences sponsored by UNESCO, the first of which was held at Addis Ababa in 1961. At this conference, priorities for educational growth were established and targets set. Three needs were given high priority status: (1) expansion at the secondary level; (2) curriculum reform, especially in terms of technical and agricultural studies; and (3) expansion of teacher-training facilities.

Table III–3 lists enrollment ratio targets which were set for all of Africa.

TABLE III–3

School Enrollment Targets for Africa

	1960/61 %	*1965/66* %	*1970/71* %	*1980/81* %
Primary	40	51	71	100
Secondary	3	9	15	23
Higher	0.2	0.2	0.4	2.0

Source: *Final Report, Conference of African States on the Development of Education in Africa* (Addis Ababa: May 1961), UNESCO and U.N. Economic Commission for Africa, Section II, p. 11.

In 1962, a conference on the development of higher education, held in Tananarive, revised somewhat the targets for that level. Table III–4 indicates the goals (in terms of enrollment ratios) that were set.

In addition, it was urged that the proportion of students in scientific and technological studies be raised from 35 per cent to 60 per cent by 1980, and that the proportion of African postsecon-

---

[23]In 1966, Kenya was said to have 150,000 primary-school leavers for whom there was no prospect of further education or paid employment. *Ibid.*, Introduction.

TABLE III–4

African Higher Educational Enrollment Targets

1965	1970	1975	1980
.35	.55	.89	1.51

Source: UNESCO, *The Development of Higher Education in Africa* (Tananarive: September 3–12, 1962; Paris: 1963), p. 22.

dary students studying abroad be reduced from 40 per cent to 10 per cent of the total by that date.[24]

As the Middle African nations seek to increase their rates of economic growth, their greatest manpower needs are at the middle and high levels. Table III–5 indicates the percentage of senior public service positions filled by Africans, in selected countries and gives some idea of the needs for high-level African manpower in many countries, as of 1960.

TABLE III–5

Percentage of Senior Public Service Positions Filled by Africans, Various Countries, 1960

Country	Percentage
Kenya	17.6
Uganda	24.6
Tanganyika	17.0
W. Nigeria	88.0
Ghana	73.3

Source: Guy Hunter, adapted from *The New Societies of Tropical Africa* (New York: Praeger, 1964), Table X.

Formal estimates of manpower needs have been made in a number of Middle African nations and related to educational output. Recent projections of future manpower requirements in Kenya and Tanzania, for example, indicate that certain existing

[24]UNESCO, *Final Report, Conference of African States on the Development of Education in Africa* (Addis Ababa: United Nations Economic Commission for Africa, May 1961), Section II, p. 11.

shortages of high-level manpower will be even more severe during the coming years. In Tanzania the number of students passing the School Certificate and Higher School Certificate examinations was 1,267 in 1961, while the annual requirements of persons with this level of education between 1962 and 1970 was estimated at 2,430. At the postsecondary-school level the annual requirement during this period was estimated at 400, while the output of Tanzanians from African and foreign universities in 1962 was only 145.[25]

Most critical is the shortage of teachers at every level and of individuals prepared for the scientific and mathematical occupations. The demand for semiprofessional persons such as technicians and nurses is also expected to increase greatly. On the other hand, the demand for high-level manpower positions open for nonspecialized degrees (business executives and administrators) was not expected to greatly exceed the supply of people capable of this work.[26]

Every Middle African nation is plagued by particular shortages in medium- and high-level manpower. Uganda, to supply the high-level manpower needed to attain its desired economic growth rate, must increase its university graduates from 4,000 in 1962 to over 22,000 by 1981. The educational problems of Uganda are even greater at the secondary level. Even Nigeria and Ghana, the only two nations with a large supply of native high-level manpower, cannot meet their needs from their own sources.

New Directions

In seeking maximum returns from educational investments, many political and educational leaders in Africa have called for different, as well as more, education. Several arguments have

[25] *The Development of Higher Education in Africa* (Paris: UNESCO, 1963), pp. 22–24.
[26] *East Africa: Kenya, Tanzania, Uganda, Study of Manpower Needs, Educational Capabilities, and Overseas Study, Report No. 3,* Study Committee on Manpower Needs and Educational Capabilities in Africa, Education and World Affairs, 1965, mimeo. Also see later studies on educational planning in Africa, published by the International Institute for Studies in Educational Planning.

been advanced, contending that education must be more directly related to national development. With the exception of recommendations related to adjustments in enrollments appropriate to manpower requirements, these arguments largely revolve around an assumed need for a new "practical" and "adapted" curriculum.

Both Africans and outside observers have strongly condemned the "literary" and "bookish" nature of colonial education. Such statements as the following are frequently found in the literature of African educators: "Our colonial masters imposed a literary education which served the purposes of civil rule"; "The school is divorced from the real world"; "Too much time is employed in the school in the mere exercise of memory, too much of a mere teaching of words, and neglect of the knowledge of things"; and "An African approach to education is needed which takes into account the facts of African life."

Specifically, the criticisms leveled at the colonial curricula have been that the language, textbooks, examinations, diplomas, and degrees offered in schools established by colonial powers were flagrantly foreign to the African setting. It has been pointed out that in the postcolonial period, for example, African school children knew more of the geography and history of England and France than of their own countries.

To replace this verbal, literary education, bold new practical curricula, adjusted to the African cultural and economic setting, have been suggested. Specifically, the advocates of a more local and more practical curriculum urge the inclusion of subjects such as bookkeeping, domestic science, handicrafts, agriculture, science, and shopwork. In addition, a number of extracurricular activities have been recommended to link the pupils' classwork to manual labor. Suggestions have been made that students should keep school gardens, be responsible for the upkeep of school buildings, and assist in community development.

One of the most articulate statements, both in terms of its trenchant criticism of the colonial heritage in education and in its radical proposals for the future, has been *Education for Self-Reliance*, by Julius Nyerere, of Tanzania. Nyerere argues that colonial education "induced attitudes of human inequality," was "based upon race," fostered the values of a different society, and simply offered too little for too few. The educational system of the future must reflect Tanzania's evolving socialist society by emphasizing "co-operative endeavour" and by stressing "concepts of equality and the responsibility to give service." Perhaps the most radical substantive change proposed by Nyerere is the explicit linking of schooling to "productive activities." Schools at all levels are to be "communities" where teachers, workers, and students plan together. "Each school should have, as an integral part of it, a farm or workshop which provides the food eaten by the community and makes some contribution to the total national income."[27]

Considering the intensity of the furor over colonial education, the effect on curriculum change has been slight. With the exception of certain experimentation in the direction suggested by Nyerere, no "revolutionary" changes have resulted. Indeed, the curriculum changes that have taken place thus far are those that logically follow achievement of national independence rather than the implementation of radically new educational principles. Textbooks are being rewritten to incorporate African history, African geography, and African art. African examinations are replacing those of Europe, and African professional educational groups are arising. Some experimentation is taking place in terms of introducing a vocational emphasis in primary schools, and new vocational secondary schools are being created. Nevertheless, African schools, like most secular schools elsewhere in the world, emphasize the three R's in the primary grades and focus essentially on academic general education at the secondary level.

Summary

The contemporary Middle African nations—both those with a long history of independence and the former colonies—view education as one of the keys to fulfilling the goals of economic growth, social justice, Africanization, and national integration. Estimates of manpower needs have been made for several nations,

---

[27] Julius K. Nyerere, *Education for Self-Reliance* (Dar es Salaam: Government Printer, 1967), p. 26.

and educational planning has been adjusted accordingly. Social justice in educational terms is viewed to mean equality of educational opportunity and a minimum education for all. While dramatic progress has been made toward the latter goal, the progress toward the former is as yet difficult to assess. The goal of Africanization—to some extent wrapped up in the goals of nation-building and social justice—has meant attempts to localize curriculum, replace "expatriate" personnel with Africans, establish "African studies" programs in universities, and encourage African art, literature, and poetry. Although certainly some of the discussion of "Negritude" and the "African personality" has been highly romantic, the closely related movements of nationalism and Africanization have assisted in making a schism between African educational systems and the European systems from which they derived.

Suggested Readings for Chapter III

American Education Commission. *Education in Africa.* New York: Phelps-Stokes Fund, 1922.

BASCOM, WILLIAM R., and MELVILLE J. HERSKOVITS, eds. *Continuity and Change in African Cultures.* Chicago: University of Chicago Press, 1959.

BURNS, DONALD G. *African Education.* London: Oxford University Press, 1965. (This is a survey of education in the Commonwealth countries.)

COLEMAN, JAMES S., ed. *Education and Political Development.* Princeton: Princeton University Press, 1965.

COWAN, L. GRAY, JAMES O'CONNELL, and DAVID G. SCANLON, eds. *Education and Nation-Building in Africa.* New York: Praeger, 1965.

FOSTER, PHILIP. *Education and Social Change in Ghana.* Chicago: University of Chicago Press, 1965.

GEORGE, BETTY. *Educational Development in the Congo.* USOE Bulletin No. 1, 1966.

HAILEY, LORD WILLIAM M. *An African Survey*, rev. ed. London: Oxford University Press, 1957.

HUNTER, GUY, ed. *The New Societies of Tropical Africa.* New York: Praeger, 1964.

International African Institute. *Social Implications of Industrialization and Urbanization in Africa South of the Sahara.* Paris: UNESCO, 1956.

KIMBLE, GEORGE H. T. *Tropical Africa*, 2 vols. New York: Twentieth Century Fund, 1960.

LEWIS, LEONARD J. *Education and Political Independence in Africa.* Edinburgh and New York: Thomas Nelson, 1963.

NYERERE, JULIUS K. *Education for Self-Reliance.* Dar es Salaam: Government Printer, 1967.

OTTENBERG, SIMON, and PHOEBE OTTENBERG, eds. *Cultures and Societies of Africa.* New York: Random House, 1960.

READ, MARGARET. *Africans and Their Schools.* London: Longmans, 1953.

SHEFFIELD, JAMES R., ed. *Education, Employment and Rural Development.* Nairobi: East African Publishing House, 1967.

SOUTHALL, AIDAN, ed. *Social Change in Modern Africa.* London: Oxford University Press, 1961.

UNESCO. *Final Report, Conference of African States on the Development of Education in Africa.* Addis Ababa: United Nations Economic Commission for Africa, 1961.

———. *The Development of Higher Education in Africa.* Paris, 1963.

CHAPTER IV

Patterns of Educational Poverty: South Asia

South Asia (comprising the modern states of India, Pakistan, and Ceylon), because of its great size and population, is frequently referred to as a subcontinent. This area, which boasts one of the oldest cultures of the world, once rivaled China in the magnificence of its literature, art, and architecture. From early times, literacy and moral education were also well developed, at least for the boys of the upper castes, and by the fourth century B.C. universities such as Taxila and Benares had become renowned as centers of learning, attracting students from throughout the East.

Over the centuries, South Asia has been subjected to an exceedingly large amount of external influence which is reflected in the pluralism of the region with regard to culture, race, language, religion, and social structure. Persians, Greeks, Afghans, Turks, Jews, and various European elements have found homes in South Asia. The three major religions—Hinduism, Islam, and Buddhism—are closely tied to nationalistic sentiments. Linguistic diversity is great and represents a continuing problem; in India alone there are some fifteen distinct languages spoken by at least a million people each.

Colonial Educational Policies

As early as the fifteenth century, the riches of the Indian subcontinent attracted adventurous European traders. By the mid-nineteenth century, when India passed from the authority of the East India Company into the control of the British government, it was considered the richest jewel in the colonial empire. British colonialism brought the entire subcontinent, from the Himalayas to Ceylon, under a single authority. Some of the profound effects of this rule on South Asia have been summarized as follows:

1. A new administrative and judicial system altered the role of the village *panchayats* (councils) and reduced the importance of law by custom.

2. The introduction of new systems of land tenure eventuated the creation of a relatively prosperous "middle" class of *zamindars* (landlords).

3. The duty-free importation of cloth and other manufactured materials led to the destruction of local handicraft industries.

4. A policy of expansion in the functions of government resulted in an increase in the activities and responsibilities of the central government. This momentum has continued since independence has been achieved.

5. The introduction of a Western educational system brought new knowledge and customs, and was instrumental in the creation of new social classes.

6. The introduction of achievement criteria in educational and occupational selection modified the old values. Caste status, kin loyalties, and village ties remained important aspects of the culture, but were increasingly forced to give ground to new, impersonal standards.

7. The introduction of the British concept of civil liberty stimulated new political goals. Through a free press and the exercise of rights of organization and assembly, South Asians frequently taunted the British with their own teachings. As has been noted, John Locke and John Stuart Mill provided more effective standards of government for educated South Asians than did the *Vedas*, the *Koran*, or the *Tripitaka*.[1]

British policies in education, as in other fields, were subject to some fluctuation and debate. Basically, the educational institutions and curricula introduced in South Asia reflected a desire to bring the presumed benefits of Christianity and Western civiliza-

[1] Myron Weiner, "The Politics of South Asia," in Gabriel A. Almond and James S. Coleman, eds., *The Politics of the Developing Areas* (Princeton: Princeton University Press, 1960), pp. 165–167.

tion to that area.[2] Particularly from the mid-nineteenth century, British policy, somewhat in contrast to its workings in Africa, came to be directed toward the establishment of a new class of South Asians familiar with Western culture and the English language. Phrased in altruistic terms, this class would serve as leaders for the masses or, more realistically, would occupy lower administrative posts in the government. In keeping with this goal, emphasis was put on secondary and higher education, and the curriculum was based on Western humanities and liberal arts.[3]

Education introduced by the British in India was accepted with more enthusiasm by the Hindus than by the Moslems. A basic reason for this was that the Moslems for centuries had had a well-organized educational system based on Islamic teachings. The mosques frequently provided the location for classes on the *Koran*, the three R's, and lectures on literacy and religious topics. This comprised an articulated system of Islamic education throughout much of South Asia; however, except for a few centers for advanced learning the results were hardly more than an oral memorization of the Koran.

Not until the Government of India Act in 1919, which gave partial control of the Central Education Department to the Indians, was serious attention given to a major expansion of educational opportunities. Even so, the two decades prior to World War II failed to bring about any dramatic increase in facilities or enrollments, although various forms of vocational education were introduced and there were several abortive local attempts at compulsory education. A partial exception was higher education, which found expansion relatively easy. The graduates from the universities formed a new class unified by a common English

[2] However, during a debate in 1793, one member of the British Parliament remarked, "We . . . lost our colonies in America by importing our education there, we need not do so in India, too." Quoted in S. N. Mukerji, *History of Education in India* (Baroda: Acharya Book Depot, 1951), p. 32.

[3] During the early decades of the 1800's when debate was being held regarding the virtues of "Oriental" versus Western learning, Thomas Babington Macaulay struck a decisive blow against the Orientalists. Macaulay argued for an education that would ". . . form a class of persons, Indian in blood and color, but English in taste, in opinions, in morals and intellect." William Theodore de Bary, ed., *Sources of Indian Tradition* (New York: Columbia University Press, 1958), p. 601.

language and by the cultural influence of their Western education. This group of Anglicized Indians, who were cut off culturally from the great masses of Indian population, nevertheless produced the ardent nationalist leaders of the independent movement.

The Social Context of Educational Development

Almost completely masked in most gross indices of South Asian development are the great intranational and international diversities in language, ideology, values, and behavior among different ethnic, religious, and social groupings. Although it is impossible to analyze in substantial detail these variations, an attempt will be made to identify those most integrally related to the problems of education.

Language Diversity

Examining first the language problem, one finds that Indians speak 1,652 dialects and that Hindi, the national language, is spoken by less than one-third of the population. Southern parts of India have refused to embrace Hindi because it is seen as just another northern technique for the domination of the south. Moreover, strong pressure is exerted by the educated elite to retain English in a position of prominence.

In Pakistan, thirty-two distinct languages are spoken, with no single language commonly spoken or understood throughout the nation. In the absence of a lingua franca, English remains the language of official use and school instruction. The Pakistani Constitution designates Urdu and Bengali as the national languages, and sets 1976 as the target for the completion of steps necessary for the replacement of English.

In Ceylon, in addition to English, two major languages, Tamil and Sinhalese (the national language), must be taken into account. After the designation of Sinhalese as the language of instruction in the lower grades in 1948, it was introduced progressively at higher levels until 1959, when it became the medium for all secondary education. Even at the university level, more and more subjects are being taught in Sinhalese and Tamil.

Religious and Value Systems

The religious and value systems of South Asia have often been noted as obstacles to social change and development. Moslem Pakistan, for example, although no longer defined as "an Islamic Republic" (as was the case in the Constitution of 1956), does include in its current constitution a statement that no law may be repugnant to Islam. The Islamic faith teaches that all believers are equal in the sight of Allah. Thus, in principle, Islam, more than Hinduism, provides the basis for a universalistic ethic conducive to a flexible social structure and individual social mobility. Actually, however, Pakistani society is rigidly stratified in terms of prestige. Tasks of manual labor are performed only by persons of low rank, and, correlatively, persons in prestigious ranks avoid tasks that do not fit in with their status. One author quotes a distinguished Moslem poet: "There are castes and sub-castes like the Hindus—surely, we have out-Hindued the Hindu himself; we are suffering from a double caste system, sectarianism, and the social caste system which we earlier learned or inherited from the Hindus."[4]

An institution that causes particular problems for Moslem women desiring to be part of the modern world is *purdah*—literally screen, or veil—which requires the seclusion of women from all males except relatives, thus not allowing participation in mixed society. Outside the home the woman must wear a *borqua*, which hides both her face and figure. *Purdah* is seen as conferring prestige, and perhaps charm and mystery. Though many girls now may be seen in Western clothes, working in offices in the cities, it has been observed that numbers of "Pakistan women have found it psychologically unendurable to leave *purdah* and enter a mixed society."[5] This form of social prejudice has inhibited school attendance for girls, either through parental preference to keep them at home or in demand for separate educational facilities.

In similar ways religious and value orientations in India and Ceylon are frequently seen as obstructing change. The Hindu

[4] As quoted by Donald N. Wilbur, *Pakistan* (New Haven: HRAF Press, 1941), p. 119.
[5] *Ibid.*, p. 156.

joint family system, while often offering succor and security to the individual, has thwarted individual striving. Capital collected by one member is placed at the disposal of all, and the goal of family unity has restricted physical and social mobility. In spite of recent weakening of this family system under the pressures of modern communication, transportation, and an urban style of living, the continuing orientation of the people to kin or caste, rather than to community or nation, continues to restrict the development of a sense of common direction.

In pointing out that "the ethnic that produced a Ben Franklin or a John D. Rockefeller has imbued relatively few persons in Ceylon," one writer summarizes the characteristics of the "status-achievement-work value matrix" of the Ceylonese as follows:

> 1. Employment in government service is of higher status than equivalent work in private enterprise.
> 2. Neither work itself nor idleness has much moral flavor; therefore, productive employment is not a value in and of itself.
> 3. Except for agriculture, manual employment of any type is denigrated, as are, to a lesser extent, entrepreneurial activities.
> 4. Thrift and savings are typically viewed as serving the purposes of consumption rather than of investment.
> 5. Wealth in land is more highly esteemed and secure than is any alternative form of investment.[6]

Several grand generalizations have been made by scholars seeking a clear distinction between the more and the less dynamic cultures of the world. Northrup, for example, has suggested a contrast between the "aesthetic" East and the "theoretic" West, and finds this to be the explanation for the persistence of traditional ways in the one, and the possibility of rapid social and technical change in the other.[7] This aesthetic quality involves an intuitive—but not speculative in the Western sense—sensitivity to the natural universe and a kind of realism: a passive acceptance of the cruelties, pains, and struggles of this world. Other authors write of the conservative effects of the philosophy of renunciation, a theme common in the literature of India, Pakistan, and Ceylon.

[6] Bryce Ryan, "Status, Achievement, and Education in Ceylon," *Journal of Asian Studies*, Vol. 20 (August 1961), p. 463.
[7] F. S. C. Northrup, *The Meeting of East and West* (New York: Macmillan, 1946).

According to the tenets of renunciation, both rich and poor are eventually expected to renounce their worldly possessions. That such is not often done is too obvious to deserve comment, but that it is sometimes done is significant. Some comfortably wealthy persons do give up their wealth and exchange their professions for more spiritual preoccupations. The fascinating experiment of Vinoba Brave, who traveled throughout the Indian countryside, urging landlords to voluntarily give up portions of their land, could have achieved its limited success only in a setting where the philosophy of renunciation had real meaning.

Others have noted spiritualism and the cyclical view of time as obstructions to change and development in South Asia. However, in spite of all that has been written about the obstructive philosophies and cultural values of Asia in general, and South Asia in particular, many situations have demonstrated that commerce, industry, and technology can prosper, and that individual desire for material comfort is far from absent. As Singer points out, material wealth and power have an important place in the Indian traditional view of life. *Artha* (wealth and power), in classic Indian literature is considered to be as important as the other three basic values: *dharma* (duty), *moksha* (liberation), and *karma* (pleasure).[8]

An empirical study of economic development in two villages in South India further suggests that villagers may discard traditional values and attitudes when it is clear to them that these severely limit economic opportunities.[9] Moreover, as other studies indicate, many South Asians readily exhibit the entrepreneurial skill and spirit considered by some economists to be the prime requisite for development. Attention could also be called to the Parsis in India who early adopted Western ways and provided leadership in commercial and industrial development.

Certainly, however, traditional value patterns have exercised a degree of constraint on educational change. Cultural values that were reflected in, and supported by, earlier South Asian educa-

---

[8] Milton Singer, "Cultural Values in India's Economic Development," *Annals*, Vol. 304, pp. 81–91.
[9] See T. Scarlett Epstein, *Economic Development and Social Change in South India* (Manchester: The University Press, 1962).

tional institutions clash with the goals of a modern, secular system. At least one segment of society, the group usually termed the modernizing elite, has rejected much of the spiritualism and inhibitions of caste and kinship structure. A modern, scientific—and for the more egalitarian members of this group—mass educational system is seen as the only legitimate kind of education to support progressive society. Yet two forces obstruct any rapid realization of such a system. First, there is still enough appeal to the spirit of tradition, even among educated South Asians, to discard easily educational arrangements that bolster the accustomed social and sex roles. Second, the force of nationalism itself has meant that effort is expended in indigenization of the educational curricula and in stimulating some rebirth of national languages and arts—actions not always reinforcing to the educational demands of development.

The evidence is inconclusive, then, as to how much drag is exerted by religious, social, and philosophical patterns. Perhaps, as Singer suggests, the linking of the concept of social service to the prevailing traditional values means that these values are now "perfectly capable of providing the spiritual incentives and disciplines of a modern industrial society."[10] However, it must also be concluded that the weight of an ascriptive social order, with its implicitly limited levels of aspiration and occupational opportunity, is still felt, particularly in the more rural areas.

Education and Social Change

Studies concerning the interaction of education with other social processes and institutions in South Asia have been neither extensive nor sophisticated. Certain fragmentary evidence can be found, however, concerning the relation of schooling and traditional values, rural and urban social structure, and certain demographic factors such as fertility rates.

Village and Urban Problems

In South Asia a large percentage of the people (in India, 82 per cent) live in villages. These economic and cultural units, with

[10] Singer, *op. cit.*, p. 86.

their caste structure and social power centered around one landlord or a very few families, remain highly conservative. A traditional and ascriptive mode of life pervades these villages. Nevertheless, obvious changes in the direction of broadening the
distribution of power, increasing intravillage and intervillage
communication, and establishing new formal organizations such
as village councils can be observed.

Education has been one factor in these changes. Opportunities
for education are much more limited, of course, in the villages
than in urban areas and tend to be distributed along class and sex
lines. A study (Table IV–1) of twelve Indian villages illustrates
this latter characteristic.

TABLE IV–1

Percentage of Literates among Different Castes
and Communities, India, *circa* 1960

Caste Group	Males	Females
1. Brahmins and other high-caste Hindus	62.7	16.9
2. Cultivating castes	29.9	8.7
3. Artisan castes	24.9	3.9
4. Backward and scheduled castes	16.5	1.4
5. Muslims	27.8	6.8
6. Christians	50.0	—
All	28.2	6.4

Source: Adapted from P.C. Joshi and M.R. Rao, "Social and Economic Factors
in Literacy and Education in Rural India," *Economic Weekly* (January 4,
1964), p. 21.

In addition to variation in educational opportunity by caste
throughout much of South Asia, the proportion of literates and
educated is higher among the younger age groups and is correlated with both social class and economic position. In one study
of primary schooling in a single Indian village, it was concluded
that there was increasing recognition of the importance of education among all social groups.[11] Nevertheless, while not always
statistically significant, enrollments did reflect the occupational
and educational status of parents. Enrollments were highest

[11] R. C. Sharma, "Socio-Economic Factors Influencing Primary School Enrollment," *Indian Journal of Social Work*, Vol. 23 (October 1962), pp. 235–241.

among children whose fathers were businessmen, and lowest among children whose parents were engaged in manual labor. Caste was found to play a particularly significant role in influencing the level of enrollment of girls, and very few of the children of artisans or "backward and scheduled castes" achieved education beyond high school.

While the results of this study follow the pattern that would be expected, one finding was somewhat surprising and may indicate a degree of social change taking place in village life. While the "Brahmins and other high-caste Hindus" are found to be more literate than other groups, the non-Brahmin cultivating castes educated approximately the same percentage of its group at the secondary level and sent an even greater percentage than did the Brahmins to higher education.

A persistent problem of the village is that it is not able to reap the full benefits from education. There is a marked tendency for educated villagers to seek better outlets for their marketable skills. This tendency is frequently manifested in migration to urban areas. A ten-city survey in India concluded that the rate of illiteracy among immigrants into urban areas was on the whole much lower than the percentage of illiteracy in the total population.[12] As Bulsara points out, the relatively well-educated migrants seem to thrive in the cities and become citizens there:

> By and large the immigrant population of cities had better education, higher overall earnings, lesser unemployment and underemployment than the resident population. This means that the immigrants are a more vital and competent part of the community. At present this phenomenon or migration is only ... from the village to the town and city and not in the opposite direction. If the village continues to replenish the urban stock of population, it cannot occur without corresponding loss to the vitality of the village, community, and the progress of rural economy.[13]

Recent years have seen a dramatic increase in the urban population of South Asia. In 1951, India had 75 cities with over 100,000 people, and in 1961 it had 117,000; Pakistan, by 1961, had also seen a sharp increase in the number of cities in this

[12]Jal F. Bulsara, *Problems of Rapid Urbanization in India* (Bombay: Popular Prakshan, 1964), p. 35.

[13]*Ibid.*, p. 140.

category. Since much of what we think of as development is associated with urbanization, the opportunities provided and problems presented by urban growth are of crucial significance to South Asia.

Probably Bulsara's study of urbanization in India is the best survey of South Asia. This study indicates that the migration to urban areas is virtually uncontrolled, and that planning in terms of municipal services, housing, and other amenities is inadequate. Little thought and study have been given to the economic, cultural, and psychological impact of urbanization on the individual or to the potential for shaping dynamic, viable, and hospitable cities. Yet, in spite of the intense poverty and planlessness so apparent in the large cities of South Asia, they offer more advantages than do the villages, not the least significant of which is education. In India, for example, the urban literacy rate for males in 1961 was 55 per cent (25 per cent for females), as compared to 24 per cent (5 per cent for females) in rural areas. In Pakistan, for the same year, urban literacy (for both sexes) was 35.8 per cent, as compared with 16.6 per cent in the rural areas in 1961. This educational inequality is further demonstrated in school attendance figures. In urban Pakistan 20.0 per cent of the young people (15–19 years of age) were attending school, as compared with 16.9 per cent in the rural areas.

Population Change and Education

One of the obstacles to both economic and educational development in South Asia, particularly in India and certain regions of Pakistan, is the large and rapidly growing population. In 1956–1957 there were about 23 million children enrolled in primary schools in India. Projections based on current rates of population growth suggest that by 1981, if it wishes to educate all primary-school-age children, that nation will have to find the resources to educate 113 million children, with a per capita income that is likely to be only about one-thirtieth that of the Western nations.[14]

[14] J. Miner and E. S. Soloman, *Implications of Population Trends for First-Level Educational Programmes* (New Delhi: UN Asian Population Conference, December 1963, mimeo).

Since, as observers have frequently concluded, urban dwellers are more positively inclined toward limiting their number of children than are villagers, rapid rates of urbanization may help to reduce the rate of population growth. Coupled with the urban style of living, or possibly even in rural areas, education may lower the birth rate substantially. One study (Table IV-2) of 1,525 Indian urban women had the following results:

TABLE IV-2

Desire for Family Limitation among 1,525 Urban Indian Women, Various Educational Levels, *circa* 1960

Educational Level	Per Cent Favoring Limitation of Family
Illiterates	44.52
Primary education	69.09
Secondary or college education	73.55

Source: Jal F. Bulsara, *Problems of Rapid Urbanization in India* (Bombay: Popular Prakashan, 1964), p. 96.

With respect to voluntary sterilization, the relation to education is even more striking. Slightly less than 10 per cent of the illiterate women in this study favored the measure, while the percentage among primary-school graduates was 27 per cent, and among secondary and college graduates nearly 61 per cent.[15] When actual fertility (rather than the attitude toward it) is considered, the evidence is less clear. In some areas actual fertility rates are found to be correlated with educational level. In central India (*circa* 1960), for example, a study of the way fertility related to educational levels showed that the number of living children among illiterate women over 45 years old was 4.7; for those with a primary education, 4.3; and high school or above, 3.2.[16] It should be noted that a marked decrease in fertility does not seem to occur until educational achievement reaches the "high school or above" level. The results of a 1951 survey in Poona district, India,

[15] *Ibid.,* p. 100.
[16] T. J. Samuel, "Social Factors Affecting Fertility in India," *The Eugenics Review.* Vol. 57 (March 1965), pp. 5–15.

showed that in Poona city only a small relationship between the educational level of the wife and fertility was ascertained, and this relationship seemed to exist only for wives who had achieved "matriculation" (ten to twelve years of school), or more. In the villages of Poona district no relationship between education and fertility was found.[17]

The relationship between level of education and attitudes toward planned family size among women is paralleled by other relationships between educational levels and modern attitudes. Educated Indians, Pakistanis, and Ceylonese enter into marriage later and generally are less inclined to accept traditional limitations on patterns of family behavior. Education, by promoting mobility and fostering economic independence, has affected the basic social unit, the family. The extended family among the educated is giving way to the nuclear; the authoritarian control of the father is weakening; and subordination of women is greatly decreasing.

Educational Planning and Priorities

Independence has brought new demands to the educational system of South Asian nations. As in other developing areas, the goals of national integration, social justice, and economic development rank foremost. Although the precise implications of these goals for education is a subject of controversy, and though experimentation still continues, certain educational priorities have been determined and large-scale educational planning is taking place.

Table IV–3 offers some partial comparative educational data on South Asia. It can be seen that, in general, Ceylon is more educationally developed than India or Pakistan. Indeed, except at the third level of education (postsecondary), Ceylon's enrollment ratios compare quite favorably with those of such European nations as Austria, France, and Italy. Pakistan rather clearly lags behind in educational development. Perhaps reflecting Moslem traditions, female education in particular is at a low level.

[17] V. M. Dandekar and Kumudini Dandekar, *Survey of Fertility and Mortality In Poona District* (Poona, India: Gokhale Institute of Politics and Economics, 1953), pp. 65, 96.

Table IV–3

South Asian Educational and Occupational Data, *circa* 1960

	India	*Pakistan*	*Ceylon*
Enrollment ratios:			
First level	62.1	37.0	90.6
Second level	23.3	10.6	39.5
Third level (higher)	3.5	0.9	0.9
Percentage of third-level students enrolled in:			
Science and technology	45.8	29.4	23.7
Humanities, arts, and law	38.0	61.3	46.9
Social sciences	8.9	3.6	2.3
Numbers per 10,000 pop. of:			
1st- and 2nd-level teachers	31.0	23.0	72.0
Engineers	3.2	—	0.9
Physicians and dentists	2.0	1.2	2.4
First-level enrollment:			
% of enrollment female	33.0	25.0	46.0
Average annual increase in enrollment 1955–1960	6.8	8.9	6.7
Second-level enrollment:			
% females in general school	24.0	19.0	NA
% females in vocational school	18.0	NA	NA
% females in teacher training	27.0	NA	35.0
Average annual rate of increase in enrollment 1955–1960	8.9	5.1	5.0
Third-level enrollment:			
% female	19.0	12.0	31.0
Average annual rate of increase, 1955–1960	5.6	NA	14.1
Percentage distribution of economically active population:			
Primary	70.0	65.0	53.0
Secondary	14.0	12.0	13.0
Tertiary	16.0	21.0	28.0
Percentage distribution of economically active population by occupation:			
Professional, technical, and related	1.9	NA	3.6
administrative, executive, and managerial	1.0	NA	NA
Clerical workers and sales	7.3	NA	11.7

Table VI-3 (*Continued*)

South Asian Educational and Occupational Data, *circa* 1960

	India	*Pakistan*	*Ceylon*
Agriculture	71.6	NA	51.2
Mining	NA	NA	0.4
Transport and communication	13.5	NA	2.5
Craftsmen and production	NA	NA	13.2
Service, sport, and recreation	4.7	NA	14.6

Source: *Educational Situation in Asia—Past Trends and Present Status*, Working
Paper, Conference of Ministers of Education and Ministers Responsible
for Economic Planning of Member States in Asia (Tokyo: UNESCO,
1965). NA indicates data not available.

In 1951, India embarked on a series of development plans. By
the end of the third Five-Year Plan (March 31, 1966), 51.5 million
children were enrolled in classes I–V. Not only does this indicate
considerable advance over the achievements of the Second Five-
Year Plan; it also represents increases in excess of the original targets established. The expansion in the field of technical education
is likewise significant. The investment in this sector increased by
seven times. The revised targets of the Third Plan called for annual admissions of 25,000 in the degree courses and 50,000 in the
diploma courses in technical fields. (Diploma courses do not
terminate in a university degree, but may be held at a university.)
Admissions during the 1965–1966 school year fell slightly short
of these targets.

The Fourth Five-Year Plan (1966–1967 to 1970–1971) calls for
continued expansion of enrollments in the age groups 6–11 and
11–14, and expansion and diversification in vocational and technical courses at the secondary level. Adult education in terms of
continuation classes, condensed courses, and extended library
services also received special attention. The target date for universal, compulsory education for the age group 6–11 is 1976.

Since independence, Pakistan has also given high priority to
planning. Under the Third Five-Year Plan (1965–1970) Pakistan
adopted a phased program for achieving universal, compulsory
primary education by 1980 (to be extended to the lower secondary

level by 1985), and for making the primary-school curriculum more "practical." At the secondary level, increased emphasis on general and vocational offerings reflects a view that secondary education is no longer merely preparation for university studies. In one Pakistani periodical an invidious comparison was drawn between the percentage of secondary-school students enrolled in technical and vocational courses in Germany (59 per cent) and in Pakistan (1 per cent). The main shortage in higher education output in terms of high-level manpower needs was interpreted to be in engineering, one of the few diploma courses in which a deficit was expected to still exist at the end of the Third Five-Year Plan.

Ceylon currently devotes a greater proportion of its annual national income (about 5 per cent) to education than does either India or Pakistan; the latter does not anticipate reaching this level of effort until 1980. However, Ceylon, perhaps because of its relatively greater achievement in education, has placed less emphasis on formal planning.[18]

A detailed tentative projection of the school system from 1960 to 1971 was prepared by the Ministry of Education, and it was proposed that a Manpower Directorate for Ceylon be established to relate education programs more closely to manpower needs, concerning which no detailed information has yet been collected. Major efforts are expected to be made toward (1) eliminating the narrowly academic nature of the educational system, thus keying it more closely to industrial needs, and (2) reducing the wastage rate at the primary level. (Currently, 50 per cent of the pupils are lost between the first and eighth year of schooling; this rate, although high, is not nearly as high as that of many Asian countries.)

In addition to separate national planning efforts there has been a substantial amount of regional planning activity in Southeast and South Asia, which has been largely focused on education at the primary level. Throughout the 1950's, a series of regional meetings helped define the dimensions of the problem of achiev-

[18] In this regard, a similarity may be noted with Mexico, an underdeveloped nation which, although placing relatively little emphasis on formal planning, has also done very well educationally compared with many other underdeveloped countries.

ing compulsory primary education and proposed programs for the accomplishment of this goal.[19]

The outgrowth of these regional meetings was the endorsement in 1960 of the Karachi Plan by seventeen Asian nations (including Ceylon, India, and Pakistan), designed to set a goal of free compulsory education of seven years' duration by 1980. Except in Ceylon, achieving this goal will require doubling the rate of expansion that has taken place in primary enrollments in South Asia during the 1950's. The targets under the Karachi Plan are set forth in Table IV–4.

TABLE IV–4

Primary Enrollments (in Millions) in 1960 and Target Figures for 1970 and 1980, Three South Asian Nations

	1960	1970	1980
Ceylon	0.8	1.9	3.7
India	33.2	71.9	119.2
Pakistan	7.4	16.3	29.4

Source: *Educational Situation in Asia—Past Trends and Present Status.* Working Paper, Conference of Ministers of Education and Ministers Responsible for Economic Planning of Member States in Asia (Tokyo: UNESCO, 1965), p. 12.

The Karachi Plan represents ambitious and possibly unrealistic aspirations. Substantial human and financial resources will be needed for its realization. Shortages of teachers, administrators, teacher educators, facilities, and materials of instruction are major obstacles. In short, a vicious circle needs to be broken: new school facilities and teacher-training institutions depend on resources resulting from increased national production, which, in turn, depends on economic development; but economic development is at least partially dependent on educational development, including primary education. Breaking the cycle in South Asia

[19]UNESCO has been deeply involved in these meetings, the first of which was called "Regional Conference on Free and Compulsory Primary Education in South Asia and the Pacific," and was held in Bombay in 1952. Subsequent meetings on this topic were held in Karachi—1956, 1959, 1960; New Delhi—1958; Manila—1960; Tokyo—1962.

and in other parts of the underdeveloped world probably will require large-scale external assistance.

The Karachi Plan, in addition to expansion of school enrollments, calls for reforms in educational goals, curricula, and teaching techniques. In general, the goal is a "progressive" education that requires a broadening of the school's functions based on the child's interests and the state's need for social responsibility and economic development.

Within the spirit (but not specifically within the stipulated plans) of the several regional meetings were a number of notable educational innovations and experiments by South Asian countries aimed at making the schools a more vital force in social change. These ranged from efforts at educational planning (commented on above) to innovations in teaching techniques. Two educational "reforms" are of particular interest because they reflect the deep concern felt by many South Asian leaders about rural poverty and village resistance to change.

The first "reform" took place in the Indian school system. To some social reformers in India, particularly Mahatma Gandhi, the numerous small villages that held the bulk of the population also held the key to national development. It followed, in the reasoning of Gandhi and others, that if education were to play a significant role in the reconstruction of society, schools must be established that would have special meaning to village life. Out of this thinking came the concept and the program of *basic education*. To Indian educators, basic education was an attempt to make instruction at once more "practical" and more "adapted" to the local scene. In actuality this usually meant the addition of a handicraft program to a regular primary-school course of study. Although the goal is to make all primary schools basic schools and to extend the concept to secondary education, by the early 1960's only 24 per cent of the primary schools were considered "basic."

Basic education is still very much the scene in India; however, there appears to be a lingering confusion about its precise purpose and content. Moreover, the supply of teachers capable of teaching crafts continues to be far less than the demand. These problems, in addition to the view of some social scientists and educators that basic education can make few serious inroads into the nation's real social and economic needs, have limited its vitality as a pedagogical experiment.

The second example was an educational experiment in Pakistan. Because of its assumptions regarding the mutual reliance of rural and urban dwellers, it is worthy of mention. In 1959, two academies were begun by the Pakistan government in support of their program of village development. The purposes are to provide Pakistani intellectuals with firsthand acquaintance with rural problems and to try to eliminate past weaknesses in the programs for village change. At the Thana Training Center, village leaders, selected by various village groups to represent them in particular fields of interest, meet with each other weekly under a teacher's guidance. The staff of the Center consists of social scientists, economists, community organizers, social psychologists, rural sociologists, and others. The major contribution of this experiment is to find out how much utility there is in having a village leader go "outside" to learn and then return to his village to teach others.[20]

Resistance to the Changing Character of Schooling

The opening of schools for large numbers of children and youth drawn from various social strata necessarily creates an educational system different in many respects from a more elitist system. For example, larger enrollments may affect administrative arrangements and teaching techniques. Second, a wider representation of social background among students may mean that new goals and values are being brought to school. These, in turn, may alter the goals and curricula of the schools, as well as the home–school relationship, and finally result in new interclass conflicts.

The response of elite groups in underdeveloped nations to the upsurge in enrollments and the opening up of what was hitherto an institution for the children of the wealthy and privileged has

[20] Henry W. Fairchild, "A New Educational Approach—the Thana Training Centre," *Jamia Education Quarterly*, Vol. 3 (July 1962), Karachi, West Pakistan (Jamia Institute of Education), pp. 12–20.

received less attention than deserved. South Asia is a good area in which to examine this phenomenon, for by the time of independence a group of comparatively wealthy landowners and merchants had evolved. To these groups was added a rising civil servant class, increasingly powerful in its own right and sought as an ally by the wealthy landowners. Educational expansion was viewed by many in these groups as meaning increased competition for prestigious jobs, adulteration of an educational pattern held dear, and ultimately the destruction of a cherished way of life.

Although it is not politic to publicize such views in South Asia, there are elitist alarms about educating too many too much. Sometimes the argument is in terms of disturbing traditional hierarchical social relationships. Brembeck quotes the feeling of one landlord: "These village boys who go off to be educated.... they no longer show proper respect for *zamindars* like myself."[21] Thus, education is felt to cause the poor to be less humble. Since their social aspirations may exceed possibilities open to them, it may also make them less content. Discontent is felt to be particularly dangerous because the lower classes now have the right to vote and thus have political power—power that is increased with literacy and oriented to ideas stemming from modern education.

Of course, opposition by elite groups to expansion of educational opportunities takes many subtle forms. Concern may be expressed for maintaining high academic standards, particularly at the upper rungs of the educational ladder. One hears that "quantity of education must not be allowed to subvert quality," or "universities must meet world standards." Or the promotion of secondary vocational or other terminal courses, ostensibly for creating more marketable skills, may actually be urged in order to preserve the elite character of higher education.

Another elitist response to educational expansion at the secondary level is the creation of new, exclusive, "quality" secondary institutions. In South Asia, residential schools of the English

[21] Cole S. Brembeck, *Rising Educational Aspirations and School Learning*, prepared for The Joint Seminar on Cultural Factors in Educational Change, University of Hawaii and Michigan State University (Honolulu: 1965, mimeo.)

"public school" variety are gaining in popularity for the privileged classes. These are frequently justified in terms of the potential of the schools to prepare leaders to fulfill the needs of the
nation for a small highly-educated core to lead the masses.

An interesting intranational regional difference reflecting the
"aristocratic-egalitarian" struggle is found in Pakistan. As Table
IV–5 shows, during the 1955–1960 period, East Pakistan spent

TABLE IV–5

Percentage of Allocations of First Pakistani Five-Year Plan to Various
Aspects of Education, East and West Pakistan, Implemented, 1955–1960

	East Pakistan %	West Pakistan %
Primary education	92	37
Secondary education	23	56
Teacher education	24	19
Technical education	96	15
Higher education	31	83

Source: Adam Curle, *Planning for Education in Pakistan* (Cambridge: Harvard
University Press, 1966), p. 54.

most of its allocated funds on primary and technical education,
while West Pakistan placed emphasis on general secondary and
higher education (largely oriented to elite groups in West Pakistan).

The foregoing discussion does not necessarily mean that
wealthy classes in South Asia all consciously plot to restrict educational opportunity to children of their own groups. First, there
are those of the upper classes who, because of a liberal persua-
sion, urge rapid expansion of educational opportunity.

Second, there are wealthy individuals whose income from industrial concerns depends on a relatively well-educated labor
force. Moreover, before the privileged are condemned, *ex
cathedra*, it should be realized that the governments of both India
and Pakistan have supported costly, low-fee residential schools,
not as a means of maintaining social class barriers, but as a way
of providing what was thought to be superior education for tal-

ented youth irrespective of social background. Of course, qualified youth tended to come to these schools mainly from the upper
classes, but this does not alter the egalitarian purpose. Finally,
arguments other than preservation of social distinction may be
presented for an elitist educational structure. Some of the theo-
rists on economic development, for example, argue that a wide
educational base on which a very narrow pyramid is built is the
best pattern to meet the technical demands of economic development.

Summary

In recent years, certain signs of economic progress have become visible in South Asia. Industrial output doubled during the
1950's (but slowed down in the early 1960's); per capita income
increased somewhat; and a structural shift in the economy fostered a movement away from the agricultural sector. On several
economic indices South Asia was equal to or above the position
of Europe at the turn of the present century. Yet the benefits of
economic and educational expansion have left unaffected many
segments of these societies. There are some indications that the
great masses of people have profited little from the growth in national production. Not only have the benefits of economic progress frequently failed to reach the rural areas but an exceedingly
high rate of population growth has eaten sharply into the increased productivity.

Educational progress has been burdened not only by a demographic structure that has a high proportion of the population
below the age of 15, but also by long-standing anti-modern traditions and even by certain aspects of the newer nationalist
traditions. High rates of illiteracy persist, yet little progress has
been made in adult education. Most analyses by either Asian or
Western educators argue for expansion at the secondary and
higher education levels only in vocational and professional
courses; yet rapid growth continues in the arts courses. Expansion of enrollments have placed such demands on the supply of
teachers that there has been little chance to achieve desirable
standards of quality of instruction. Certain aspects of the new

nationalism, which accepted many traditional values and was
ambivalent in its commitment to a secular, liberal society, have
become increasingly apparent, especially among the students and
younger political leaders of Ceylon and India. And the "philosophy" of teaching has been reflected in an aloof and disengaged
manner on the part of many teachers which has discouraged
initiative and inquiry on the part of students. One hears, for example, that Indian universities are institutions "where the de-
moralized teach the disgruntled."

On the more positive side has been a continued and increasingly realistic commitment to education by national leaders.
Indian government spokesmen, for example, have frequently
claimed that trained manpower is the most fundamental of all the
resources needed for development—a view echoed by Pakistani
officials. Ceylon, more educationally advanced, has been able to
see many of its educational targets clearly and has begun to lay
plans for extension of compulsory education and a general upgrading of the quality of instruction.

Suggested Readings for Chapter IV

BULSARA, JAL F. *Problems of Rapid Urbanization in India.* Bombay:
Popular Prakashan, 1964.
CORMACK, MARGARET L. *She Who Rides a Peacock: Indian Students and
Social Change.* New York: Praeger, 1961.
CURLE, ADAM. *Planning for Education in Pakistan.* Cambridge: Har-
vard University Press, 1966.
DE BARY, WILLIAM THEODORE, ed. *Sources of Indian Tradition.* New
York: Columbia University Press, 1958.
Educational Situation in Asia—Past Trends and Present Status. Work-
ing Paper, Conference of Ministers of Education and Ministers Re-
sponsible for Economic Planning of Member States in Asia. Tokyo:
UNESCO, 1965.
EPSTEIN, T. SCARLETT. *Economic Development and Social Change in
South India.* Manchester: The University Press, 1962.
India: *Report of the Education Commission 1964–66: Education and Na-
tional Development.* New Delhi: Ministry of Education, Govern-
ment of India, 1966.
India: *Review of the Third Five-Year Plan.* New Delhi: Ministry of
Publications, Government of India, n.d.
India: *The Teacher Today and Tomorrow.* New Delhi: Ministry of Edu-
cation, Government of India, August 1966.

MUKERJI, SHRIDHAR NATH. *Education in India: Today and Tomorrow,* 4th ed. Baroda: Acharya Book Depot, 1960.

MYRDAL, GUNNAR. *Asian Drama.* Vol. III. New York: Pantheon, 1968.

NAIK, J. P. *Educational Planning in India.* New Delhi: Allied Publishers, 1965.

NAIR, KUSUM. *Blossoms in the Dust—The Human Factor in Indian Development.* New York: Praeger, 1962.

NURALLAH, SYED, AND J. P. NAIK. *A History of Education in India.* New York: Macmillan, 1951.

CHAPTER V

Patterns of Educational Poverty: Latin America

Latin America, like the other underdeveloped regions, offers great intraregional contrasts in most of the common indices of development. Moreover, although united by Latin culture, there are marked cultural differences among the twenty nations. In Argentina and Uruguay, for example, the populations are almost entirely of European origin. On the other hand, in Central America, Mexico, and the Andean Highlands, large Indian populations may be found whose way of life predates European settlement. Thus, there exist side by side in Latin America Euro-American, Indo-American, and, in a few cases, Afro-American cultures. As might be expected, the nations with larger "European" populations are at more advanced stages of development than those where a strong Indian culture exists.

Colonial Educational Policies

By the middle of the seventeenth century, Latin America was firmly under the rule of Spain and Portugal, whose colonial policies were based on the desire to make economic profit, to spread Christianity to the Indians, and to create a culture in the New World as nearly like that of the homeland as possible. Although many of the Indians had a highly developed civilization, they were largely regarded as savages. Their institutions were destroyed, and their language and religion replaced by those of the Iberian Peninsula.

In Spanish America, the colonial government was a well-organized, highly-centralized institution that owed allegiance to the Spanish Crown and the Catholic Church. Cultural values of the Old World combined with race to determine economic opportunity and social prestige, and the resulting class lines were rigidly maintained. The Caucasians formed the upper class, which controlled all highly productive economic enterprises. The elite of this class were those born in Spain (*peninsulares*), and to them were reserved almost all the leadership positions in both government and Church. Next in the hierarchy were the *criollos*, or persons born in Spanish America of European ancestry. The *mestizos* (Caucasian-Indian) occupied an upper lower-class role as farmers or small entrepreneurs, while the Indians and Negroes in the lowest social positions supplied agricultural, mining, and domestic labor. The latter class were slaves in the early period, and feudal peons later. Feudalism and paternalism characterized the relationship between the upper and lower classes.

Portuguese America (Brazil) followed Spanish America's general pattern of colonialism. However, neither the Church nor the government was as strong or well organized. Due to Portugal's interest in more profitable colonies elsewhere, much was left to the individual initiative of the colonists in Brazil. The result was the development of a strong familistic feudalism under which the large plantation owner was virtually the center of all power and allegiance in his particular area. In further contrast to Spanish America, Brazilian class and racial lines were less rigidly drawn, and little attention was given to distinguishing between the *peninsulares* and the colonial-born Europeans.

Education in colonial Latin America was the responsibility of the Church. A few Catholic educators urged progressive practices, such as the establishment of common schools to serve all people, regardless of class; the introduction of scientific methods; and the development of closer ties between the school and community. However, education on the whole was patterned on the class-conscious, multiple-track system found in Spain and Portugal. Education for the lower classes was a duty of the local priests. In some cases, schools which offered instruction in crafts, Spanish, and religion were provided for Indians; more often, instruction in the rudiments of religion was considered sufficient. For the *mestizo* and mulatto, schools provided training in various trade skills, the three R's, and religion. For the upper classes, institutions offered essentially the same literary and professional curricula as were found in Europe.

The most significant contribution to education was made by the Jesuits, who established a large number of *colegios* which became models for much of contemporary Latin American secondary education, and offered a traditional liberal arts curriculum to the Spanish, Portuguese, and *criollo* elite. Although the best higher education was believed to be obtained only in Europe, important universities were established (often by the Jesuits) in Spanish America.[1] These institutions, which traced their traditions to the great Spanish universities and through these to the twelfth-century University of Bologna, became, in the New World, primarily theological in character. The early Latin American universities were strongly scholastic, and less influenced than the universities of Northern Europe (the source of many of the traditions in North American universities) by the philosophy and letters of the Renaissance and the Reformation. Moreover, in contrast to the northern New World where the study of arts and sciences became preparatory to professional studies in Latin America, arts and sciences (or philosophy and letters) became an alternative to the professional studies.

Obstacles to Educational Development

The heritage of colonialism and cultural changes during the last century and a half of political sovereignty have contributed to three significant and, to some extent, distinctive obstacles to Latin American development.

The "Indian" Problem

To foster either the social or the economic goals of development, the large mass of Indians (or *mestizos*, who are most often largely Indian in culture) must become participating members of the national society. Wagley and Harris, in distinguishing nine significant Latin American subculture types, include "Tribal

---

[1] Due largely to the expulsion of the Jesuits in the eighteenth century, no universities were established in Brazil during the colonial period.

Indian," "Modern Indian," and "Peasant Type." The Tribal Indian subculture is comprised of the few remaining aboriginal people, while "Modern Indian" refers to a fusion of aboriginal and Iberian institutions and cultural patterns. The "Peasant Type" subculture includes such horticultural peoples as the *mestizos* in Mexico, the *Ladinos* in Guatemala, and the *Cholos* in Peru.[2] Although these groups are culturally distinct, they are characterized by large numbers of illiterates, lack of facility in the national language, and their own traditional value patterns. These aspects of Indian life create serious communication and other difficulties in efforts at national development.

Population Change

A second obstacle is the burden of a rapid population expansion, owing to an extremely high birth rate and a decreasing death rate. In the less modern population groups, lack of education and primitive economic and social conditions maintain the high birth rates, and population increase is curbed only by the high incidence of infant mortality. In the few advanced urban centers a modest drop in the birth rate has been more than compensated for by the decrease in the infant mortality rate, owing to improved hygienic conditions. The problem of population in Latin America is not so much one of absolute numbers, but rather a rate of growth that often outruns and inhibits development gains.

Shifts in population may hinder as well as assist social change. Migration of the farm population to the large cities, for example, usually takes place before being justified by the mechanization of agriculture and the technical and industrial development of the cities. The result is a growing mass of unproductive urban poor, and may also mean a drop in agricultural productivity as the more advanced persons migrate to urban centers.

Inhibitive Value Structure

Latin American societies were formed when feudal institutions and ideas were still strong in Spain and Portugal. For example,

[2]Charles Wagley and Marvin Harris, "A Typology of Latin American Subcultures," *American Anthropologist*, Vol. 57, No. 3 (June 1955), pp. 428–449.

"family" remains an extremely strong criterion for social position; paternalistic relationships and attitudes persist on the *latifundio* (landed estate), and social-class lines are rigid and in part racially defined. It has been further suggested that the level of cooperation—or its preconditions, faith and trust in others—may be too low in parts of Latin America to allow business, governmental, or educational institutions to function efficiently.[3] The assumption underlying this argument is that development demands flexibility of operation and organizational growth; these in turn depend on decentralization and delegation of authority and successful interorganizational relations, all of which imply ability to cooperate in a predictable way.

One comparative study of the prevalence of "faith in people" in populations in Lima, Peru, and the United States found, for example, that in the Peruvian sample only 34 per cent agreed that "most people can be trusted," while the response in the United States sample was 79 per cent. Further, only 8 per cent of the Peruvian sample (as compared to 28 per cent in the United States sample) disagreed with the statement: "If you don't watch yourself, people will take advantage of you."[4]

Additional obstacles in Latin America, common to most developing areas, can be identified as (1) the relative lack of a middle stratum of society and the way of life associated with it and (2) a failure to assimilate many modern ideas because of an extreme sensitivity to foreign intervention into national life. These problems and obstacles do not exist to the same degree in all Latin American nations. The nations that are predominantly Euro-American, such as Argentina, Uruguay, and Chile, are the most economically advanced in Latin America, with generally higher per capita income, smaller proportions of their population engaged in farming, higher consumption of electrical power, and higher literacy. Problems of communication and cultural integration are relatively minor in these nations. On the other hand, nations less "white" and largely dependent on agriculture, such as

[3] Ralph Beals, "Social Stratification in Latin America," *American Journal of Sociology*, Vol. 58 (1953), p. 339.

[4] William F. Whyte, "High Level Manpower for Peru," in Frederick H. Harbison and Charles A. Myers, eds., *Manpower and Education: Country Studies in Economic Development* (New York: McGraw-Hill, 1965), p. 66.

Guatemala, Haiti, and Honduras, tend to rank low on development indices.

Development Goals and Educational Change

Since 1956, the idea of national and regional educational planning has been gaining favor in Latin America. Essentially, educational plans are viewed as a means for more rational determination of educational priorities. From the standpoint of overall national goals they are seen as programs for accelerating the growth of the human attributes deemed necessary for economic and social development. Few voices in contemporary Latin America are raised in opposition to the claims that more and better education is requisite to the achievement of national goals.

Educational Planning

A series of education "task forces" of the Organization of American States over the last decade have furthered the concept of planning and have attempted to set quantitative educational targets based on the demographic, financial, socioeconomic, and pedagogical factors involved. In effect, these task forces recommended increased output of the educational systems at all levels and diversification of secondary education to increase the vocational offerings. At the higher level they urged that the most rapid expansion be sought in technical and scientific fields. (In 1960, 60 per cent of Latin American university graduates received degrees in medicine, law, education, or the humanities, while only 40 per cent obtained degrees in the social sciences, engineering and technical studies.) That the general recommendations for enrollment expansion were in keeping with recent educational trends can be demonstrated by Table V-1.*

As a further index of educational effort, Latin American nations have dramatically increased the size of education budgets over the past decades. Data are available on the amount of money devoted to education by most Latin American nations in 1938, 1953, and 1957, converted to constant currency. Using 1953 expenditures as an index (1953 = 100.0), the range in median increase between 1938 and 1957 was from 13.05 to 163.05, with the

TABLE V–1

Primary and Secondary Enrollment as Percentage of
Appropriate Age Groups (5–14 and 15–19) in
Thirteen Latin American Countries

a. *Number of Latin American countries having a primary enrollment ratio of:*

Year	20–39	40–59	60+
1950	3	5	5
1960	1	5	7

b. *Number of Latin American countries having a secondary enrollment ratio of:*

Year	0–14	15–24	25–40
1950	6	6	0
1960	0	7	5

Source: *Report on the World Social Situation* (New York: United Nations, 1963),
pp. 65, 67.

smallest increase going from 23.6 to 126.9 (Panama) and the
greatest from 1.3 to 579.8 (Paraguay). The 1953–1957 increases—
considering the short time span—are even more dramatic. The
median nation, Colombia, was spending 1.6 times as much money
on education in 1957 as in 1953. The range again was quite large,
going from Haiti (1.2 times as much) and Panama (1.3) to Brazil
(5.2), Chile (5.5), and Paraguay (5.8).[5]

Yet growth in educational expenditure, and expansion of educational enrollments, whether planned or unplanned, in themselves tell little about many of the subtle problems facing the
educators and planners. How was the existing educational effort
linked, for example, with such critical development problems as
a population explosion and backwardness in vast rural areas?
And what were the crucial intra-educational problems that ob-
structed a higher quality of educational output?

[5]Gino Germani, in Egbert de Vries and José M. Echavarria, eds., *Social Aspects of Economic Development in Latin America* (Paris: UNESCO, 1963), p. 293.

Population Change and Education

There is an obvious connection between the structure, size and growth of a nation's population and its problems in education. Less clear are the linkages between education and population control. Generally, it is assumed that education has a depressing effect on fertility, and in some underdeveloped countries certain educational efforts directed specifically at fertility decrease have had remarkable success.

The data available on the correlations between fertility rates and educational achievements offer an inconclusive picture. A survey carried out in Santiago, Chile, in 1959, indicated that education had a depressing effect on fertility within given economic classes, being more pronounced in the poorer and richer classes than in the middle groups.[6] The survey also indicated that education was more significantly associated with differences in fertility rates than was the frequency of church attendance. But in a study of twenty Latin American countries, it appeared that urbanization was far more significant than education as a factor in reducing fertility. When urbanization was held constant, the correlation between lower fertility and education fell sharply to insignificant levels; but when education was held constant, there was only a small decline in the correlation between urbanization and lower fertility.[7]

An extensive study of differences between political sub-units within each of eleven Latin American countries has been recently completed. No single or consistent pattern can be found in these data,[8] but it appears that in countries that are both economically and educationally well advanced, such as Argentina, there is more likelihood of finding a strong inverse relationship between educa-

[6] Leon Tabah and Raul Samuel, "Preliminary Findings of a Survey on Fertility and Attitudes toward Family Formation in Santiago, Chile," in Clyde V. Kiser, ed., *Research in Family Planning* (Princeton: Princeton University Press, 1962), p. 282.

[7] Material made available by J. Mayone Stycos, Cornell University, in R. M. Bjork, *Education and Population* (Syracuse: Syracuse University, 1966, mimeo) pp. 16–17.

[8] *Ibid*, pp. 22–24.

tion and fertility than in countries like Bolivia, which are relatively underdeveloped educationally and economically.

It can also be noted in these studies that when urbanization is controlled, the correlations between educational attainment and fertility rates drop significantly. A tentative conclusion might be that the likelihood of education's having a depressing effect on fertility rates is increased when the nation in question is somewhat urbanized and already has a sizable proportion of the population with at least a primary-school education.

The pressures of population growth on education must become a major concern for educational planners in Latin America. For example, in 1960, the secondary-school enrollment ratios ranged from 42 per cent in Uruguay to 4 per cent in Haiti. It has been estimated that merely to hold their 1960 ratios will require, by 1980, over 100 per cent expansion of enrollments in Venezuela, Mexico, El Salvador, Honduras, and Panama. The advantage of a lower birth rate is demonstrated by Uruguay, where the estimated necessary expansion is less than 5 per cent.[9]

The estimates of additional teachers needed because of increases in school-age population likewise offer a serious but varied picture. Assuming a pupil-teacher ratio of 25, and enrollment ratio of 98 per cent at the primary-school level by 1980 would require, for example, over 700,000 new teachers for Brazil and nearly 500,000 new teachers for Mexico. The proportionate increases for such nations as Honduras, Haiti, and Guatemala (countries with low enrollment ratios and high birth rates) would be even greater.[10]

Financing such educational growth will clearly be a major concern for years to come. Assuming that the budget for primary and secondary education will grow in proportion to the total population, and given the assumptions of enrollment increases already noted, the percentage increase in expenditure per student ranges from a low of 54 in El Salvador to a high of 124 in Costa Rica.[11]

[9]Jorge V. Arevalo, "Population Growth and Education," in J. Mayone Stycos and Jorge Arias, eds., *Population Dilemma in Latin America* (Washington: Potomac Books, Inc., 1966), pp. 133–134.

[10]*Ibid.*, p. 136.

[11]*Ibid.*, p. 140. Data available only for Argentina, Chile, Colombia, Costa Rica, Cuba, Ecuador, El Salvador, Mexico, Nicaragua, and Venezuela.

Rural Development and Education

As in other underdeveloped regions, the villages and rural areas of Latin America have advanced least along the path to development. It has been the hope of many political and educational leaders that literacy and educational programs would act to accelerate social change. However, considerable doubt about the school's effectiveness in this capacity has been expressed by social scientists who have observed at first hand the operation of Latin American village schools. A cultural gulf frequently exists between the teacher and the villager. The teacher lacks a sufficient understanding of the local culture to allow him to play a mediating or "broker" role between local and national interests. Further, when the population of the villages is primarily Indian, a language difference frustrates communication with school authorities, and promotes distrust. While there is some evidence that better schools and better-trained teachers can provide stimulation for change, the schools that presently exist in rural Latin America generally are not agents for change. After a study of villages and village schools in Asia and Latin America, Nash concludes the following:

(1) It is change in the economic, religious, and interpersonal relations on the local and regional levels which is antecedent to change in the educational system.

(2) Local schools tend to be conservative agents, transmitting values that reinforce local tendencies toward stability.

(3) Education becomes a force for social change only when the process of social change is well underway.[12]

Although crash literacy and special rural educational programs rarely are a vital force for rural transformation, Nash argues that schools maximize their influence for change when they are a part of a conscious governmental effort to effect change in all sectors.

A further complication in considering education's contribution to rural development in Latin America has been the exodus of the better-educated from rural settings. Not only are there fewer and less qualified schools in rural areas, but students who leave the

[12] Manning Nash, "The Role of Village Schools in the Process of Cultural and Economic Modernization," *Social and Economic Studies*, Vol. 14, No. 1 (March 1965), p. 143.

region for postprimary education elsewhere are unlikely to return. A survey of the more rural and poorer states in Mexico in 1960, for example, indicated the inability of these areas to fill the few existing jobs calling for high educational qualifications with persons who had the appropriate backgrounds. "In 1960 the number [of people] employed in the high level categories was more than $2\frac{1}{2}$ times larger than the number with 12 years of education or more."[13] Only in the lowest skill levels do the rural areas have the necessary manpower resources, and many of these are underemployed.

Dissemination of Education

Enrollment ratios in 1960 for Latin America as a whole are estimated as follows:

Primary education (7–12) . . . . 78.5 per cent
Secondary education (13–19) . . . . 15.5 per cent
Higher education (20–24) . . . . 3.1 per cent

To further clarify the picture, however, it is necessary to realize that only a fraction of the students are expected to complete the level of education in which they are enrolled. At the respective educational levels the estimated completion rates in 1960 were 4 per cent, 5 per cent, and 10 per cent.[14]

One persistent problem in the dissemination of education in Latin America is the wide social-class and regional variations in educational opportunities, and the level of education attained. Legislation in most Latin American nations emphasizes the right, without discrimination, to free, compulsory, primary education. Secondary and higher education likewise are frequently free, and students from poorer families often are exempted from whatever fees are levied.[15] Yet the extent to which Latin Americans have desired, or have been able, to take advantage of available educa-

---

[13] Charles Nash Myers, *Education and National Development in Mexico* (Princeton: Princeton University, 1965), p. 60.

[14] Sylvain Lourie, "Education for Today or Yesterday," in Raymond F. Lyons, ed., *Problems and Strategies of Educational Planning* (Paris: UNESCO, IIEP, 1965), pp. 31–32.

[15] De Vries and Echavarria, *op. cit.*, p. 280.

tional opportunities varies considerably. An attempt now will be made to summarize the variation in dissemination of schooling and to provide an analysis of the reasons for existing disparities.

The conditions that limit the spread of schooling throughout the people of Latin America are basically nonpedagogical in nature. Lack of parental financial means, need for child labor, and lack of faith in the rewards of schooling combine to foster poor school attendance and high school dropout rates. Moreover, there is some evidence that the social supports to education —the social conditions that make it possible and desirable for more children to attend school longer—are not rapidly being provided. For example, in Brazil, between 1948 and 1958 there was no general improvement in school attendance for the relevant age groups. The data in Table V–2 reveal this failure to improve.

The rural-urban differences in educational levels found in most underdeveloped nations may also be found in Latin America. Argentina, Uruguay, and Chile are among the most urbanized

TABLE V–2

Percentage of Appropriate Age Group in
Each of the First Eight Years of School,
Brazil, 1948 and 1958

Grade	*Per Cent of Age Group in School Grade*	
	1948	*1958*
I	46.2	41
II	17.3	21
III	15.4	15
IV	9.5	10
V	4.2	5
VI	3.5	4
VII	2.7	2.5
VIII	1.2	1.5

Source: J. Roberto Moreira, in Egbert de Vries
and José M. Echavarria, eds., *Social
Aspects of Economic Development in
Latin America* (Paris: UNESCO, 1963),
pp. 310–311.

and highly-educated nations. On the other hand, Ecuador, Honduras, Paraguay, and Peru all have low urbanization indices and are among the lowest in level of education. Intranational data indicate that urban areas have higher school attendance and lower dropout rates than rural areas. One interesting exception to the close correlation between urbanization and educational development is found in Costa Rica, a nation with a high percentage of rural population but also high level of education. Its small geographic area, political stability, high proportion of European-derived people, and high expenditures on education may have contributed to make Costa Rica a special case.

Any discussion of urbanization and education should be further qualified. Urban growth in itself may not be sufficient to generate expansion in educational opportunities. Usually, however, urbanization resulting from industrialization and modernization of agriculture (as is found, for example, in Southern Brazil) implies a demand for skills necessitating an educated labor force. This type of urbanization implies a style of living of which schooling is an integral part.

A second persistent problem, mentioned earlier in this chapter, concerns the inhibitive effects on development of certain values. An important illustration of this in the field of education would be the much-discussed preference of more advanced students for white-collar work. The result of a questionnaire on values given to high-school students in Peru is enlightening in this regard. Students were asked: "If you had to choose between two jobs earning an equal amount in either one, but in one you would be an *obrero* (blue-collar worker) and the other an *empleado* (white-collar worker), which job would you prefer?" As expected, most of the students preferred white-collar employment. For those who chose this category an attempt was made to measure the intensity of the preference, which turned out to be somewhat surprising: 35.6 per cent of the students replied that, despite the size of potential salary benefits, they would never become blue-collar workers. Another one-third of the sample said they would consider blue-collar work only at a wage differential that was clearly unrealistic.[16]

[16] Whyte, *op. cit.*, pp. 51, 52.

Considering the whole Latin American region, the degree to which Latin Americans differ in their acquisition of the values supportive of social change and development is difficult to determine. In one study of Argentina, Chile, Brazil, and Mexico, data on "development values" (among other variables) were sought. This study concluded that generally the Argentines and Chileans interviewed had incorporated more actively the values supportive of life in more complex and developed social environments than had the Brazilian and Mexican samples.[17] Yet, as the author of the study points out, identification with development values varied greatly intranationally according to the occupation and social class to which individuals belonged.

While the inhibitive effects of certain value orientations on schooling are obvious, the effects of schooling on value and behavior change are subject to debate. At the very least, the schools in Latin America can have, at some point, an important indirect role to play. By imparting knowledge, attitudes, and skills, schools can prepare youth for a specific occupation and a suitable place in the social milieu. The occupational group and social setting may in turn prove exceedingly instrumental in helping the individual further acquire modern values.

Problems of Secondary Education

In this section and the one following, an arbitrary selection has been made of the secondary and higher levels of education in Latin America in order to focus more specifically on the problems and direction of educational change.

The most highly esteemed of Latin American secondary schools are those whose programs are primarily academic in nature—the *colegios* or *liceos*. The courses of study in these government- and church-controlled institutions include the usual range of subjects in the humanities and the social and physical sciences, as are typically found throughout the world. However, due to a bookish tradition, a lack of facilities, and inadequately trained teachers, frequently little in the way of laboratory or other applied experiences is provided.

[17] Kalman H. Silvert and Frank Bonilla, *Education and the Social Meaning of Development* (New York: American Universities Field Staff, 1961), p. 150.

Other factors limiting the efficiency of secondary instruction can be identified. The commonly-held community view of the teacher as an agent of the government may hinder his being accepted, and frustrate easy teacher-student communication. The part-time nature of the teaching job (most teachers hold additional positions) and high teacher turnover further detract from the quality of instruction. Last, the deleterious effects of the absence of any concept of guidance should be mentioned.

On the more positive side, certain trends and experimentation at the secondary level hold much promise. One distinguished Latin American educator lists a number of hopeful trends, including "the introduction of elective and differentiated courses in most countries; the creation of comprehensive high schools in others; the growth and diversification of technical education at the secondary level; and the setting up of experimental programs or pilot projects for the reorganization of the curricula."[18]

The major inadequacies in secondary education must be seen in the context of the social milieu. Concern is frequently expressed over the relationship between social class and educational attainment in Latin America. For example, in Table V–3, data from Buenos Aires show the impact of social origin on the question of who attains an education.

The relationship between the occupational level of the father and the educational level attained by the son is so evident in this large urban center that it might be expected to be at least equally marked throughout Latin America. Unfortunately, there are little existent data in most of Latin America about the extent to which education is tied to family status.

Secondary-school students, whether in public or private schools, aspire strongly to a higher education—a condition that tends to exist, although to somewhat less extent, in the vocational and technical schools. That such aspirations are often unrealistic is seen from the small percentage of students who succeed in gaining admittance to universities. Data from Chile, for example, indicate that in recent years one-half or less of the students passed

---

[18] Irma Salas, "Secondary Education in Latin America," *Phi Delta Kappan*, Vol. 45, No. 4 (January 1964), pp. 175–176.

TABLE V–3

Level of Educational Attainment by Occupational Class
of Father, Buenos Aires, 1960–1961

	Educational Level Attained by Sons			
Occupational Level of Father	Without Education %	Primary Incomplete %	Primary Complete %	Secondary Complete or Incomplete %
I Unskilled manual	7.0	49.9	33.4	2.7
II Semiskilled and skilled manual	4.0	30.0	48.4	3.1
III Lower white-collar	4.2	24.9	41.6	6.7
IV Middle white-collar	0.0	12.5	40.4	13.2
V Technical and professional	1.3	6.6	28.9	18.4
VI Medium size businessmen and free professionals	3.7	19.0	28.2	19.0
VII Large industrialists and high officials	0.0	0.0	3.3	50.0

Source: Gino Germani, *La Mobilidad en la Argentina*, Servicio de Documentación de Sociología, Publicación Interno No. 60, Instituto de Sociología, Facultad de Filosofía y Letros, Universidad de Buenos Aires, 1961, p. 20.

the *bachillerato*, the secondary-school leaving examination, necessary for admission to higher education.

The attrition rate within the secondary program also tends to be great. In 1960, it was estimated that in Chile only 24 per cent of those who entered the first grade had finished the sixth year. Other Latin American nations have reported similarly high attrition rates, with typically only 2 to 6 per cent of the students who began the first year of primary school completing secondary education. It has been estimated that because of wastage rates, the cost per graduated student in secondary education in Latin America has been increased three times.

It is clear that secondary education has not been influenced sufficiently by the labor market. The output of the secondary schools is not meeting the needs for middle-level manpower, such as subprofessionals, technicians, administrative assistants, and the like. In Peru, planners have called for a massive effort at the secondary and post secondary school levels to train the needed technical personnel. It has been estimated that over 40 percent of the new entrants to the labor force between 1960 and 1980 will be graduates of vocational secondary schools or technical colleges. In Mexico, a manpower survey undertaken between 1955 and 1957 by the Banco de Mexico, which sampled one out of every twenty-two manufacturing institutions, found "for every five professionals employed in manufacturing there was only one subprofessional, an inversion of what is generally considered the optimum ratio."[19] The most vocal complaints about manpower shortages came from managers of such industries as automobile construction and assembly, electrical machinery and appliances, nonferrous metals, iron and steel, and other "mechanical" industries which have been expanding most rapidly in the past decade. Myers attributes this shortage to (1) lack of attention by the government to secondary education and (2) the low prestige of non-university preparatory education, which inhibits students from entering training programs for such occupations.

Problems at the University Level

In recent years, the Latin American universities have been the focus of considerable criticism in the educational literature of both North and South America. The university is usually seen as playing less of a role than it might in supporting the developmental goals of the nations. Without suggesting that these problems exist to the same extent throughout Latin America, or that they are as prevalent now as a few years ago, the following problems may be identified.

1. The university trains students primarily in the humanities

[19] Myers, *op. cit.*, pp. 121–122.

and the traditional professions of law and medicine and gives relatively little attention to the physical sciences, social sciences, applied sciences, or the newer professions. Judged in terms of current or foreseeable employment needs, it is clear that in several nations an excess of lawyers exists, but it is more difficult to validate other criticisms. The accusation that the university curricula are not geared to the needs of societies bent on technical and industrial development frequently has been based on comparison of enrollments in the various engineering and technical courses with those of the more developed nations. Data (*circa* 1960) indicate that the proportion of university students enrolled in engineering, for example, was considerably less in most Latin American nations than in Sweden, the United Kingdom, or West Germany. Considering the level of industrialization in Latin America, this fact in itself is not disturbing. However, scattered estimates of manpower needs in several nations suggest that the supply of engineers is not adequate even for Latin America's level of development.

2. The university draws students primarily from, and therefore caters unduly to, the upper social classes. To some extent this accusation is borne out by the facts. The case of Brazil, in 1955, indicated in Table V–4, could be replicated in other Latin American nations. Although the upper class dominates the university, there is a sizable number of students from lower middle-class backgrounds in the more technical institutions of higher learning, many of whom, upon graduating, will achieve higher social status.

3. The facilities of the universities are inadequate, particularly in terms of laboratories and other specialized teaching devices. This shortage is aggravated by repetition of course offerings among autonomous faculties and institutes within a university. Thus elementary instruction in chemistry or physics may be given independently in Faculties of Engineering, Philosophy, Industrial Chemistry, Pharmacy, Dentistry, and Medicine, with each faculty maintaining its own laboratories, equipment, and library. Moreover, there is a severe shortage of professors in many academic specializations, and, due to low salaries and lack of tenure arrangements, most of the faculty are on a part-time basis.

TABLE V–4

Social-Class Origins of Students in Three Institutions of
Higher Education, Brazil, *circa* 1955
(percentage distribution)

	INSTITUTIONS		
Class	A	B	C
Upper	74	10	7
Upper middle	—	41	29
Lower middle	16	37	48
Upper working	8	12	16
Lower working	2	—	—

Source: Robert Havighurst and Roberto Moreira, *Society and Education in Brazil*
(Pittsburgh: University of Pittsburgh Press, 1965), p. 104. Institution A
is the University of São Paulo; B is the Technological Institute of Aero-
nautics at São José dos Campos (São Paulo); and C is the School of
Architecture of the University of Brazil. Ratings of social status are
based on occupation and income of father. All data are for the mid-
1950's.

4. University autonomy frustrates cooperation between the
universities and national governments.   Since the university
reform movement, originating in 1918, most Latin American
universities have zealously maintained their freedom from state
interference. While the desire for autonomy may have been a
justifiable moral response to crude attempts at governmental
coercion, a militant isolationism on the part of the universities
limits their contributions to national development. The mutual
benefits resulting from the direct contact that has been established
between university and government (as in the state universities
of Mexico and in the Universidad de Oriente) would argue
strongly for continued explorations of means for communication
between the two institutions.[20]

The image of the Latin American university as an institution
catering only to the upper classes and providing leisurely aca-

[20] For a particularly strong indictment of the inefficiencies and inadequacies
of Latin American universities, see Russell C. Davis, "Prototypes and Stereotypes
in Latin American Universities," *Comparative Education Review*, Vol. 9, No. 3
(October 1965), p. 281.

TABLE V–5

Data on Educational Orientations of People with Higher Education,
Argentina, 1946–1950 and 1956–1960, and Peru, 1950–1960

A.

*Graduates of All Argentine Universities in the Ten Most Numerous
Careers (in Percentages)*

Years	Doctors	Lawyers	Engineers	Dentists	Pharmacists
1946/50	25.4	15.6	14.2	10.6	8.7
1956/60	23.4	14.8	18.7	9.2	6.9

Years	Accountants	Notaries	Midwives	Architects	Agricultural Engineers
1946/50	8.2	8.7	2.3	2.6	3.7
1956/60	10.1	4.6	6.0	4.1	2.2

B.

University Enrollments in Peru by Areas of Specialization

Year	Letters	Law	Sciences, Preparatory	Medicine	Obstetrics	Dentistry
1950	10.35	9.51	14.56	16.02	3.81	3.61
1960	16.96	11.13	14.33	6.60	.97	3.37

Year	Veterinary Medicine	Pharmacology and Biochemistry	Biological Sciences	Physical Science and Math	Geology
1950	.75	3.66	.82	.97	.56
1960	.78	3.69	.73	.52	1.37

Year	Agronomy	Chemistry and Chemical Engineering	Economics and Com. Sciences	Engineering
1950	3.35	5.78	9.50	6.44
1960	3.05	1.72	14.61	12.69

Year	Journalism	Education	Others
1950	1.20	7.61	1.50
1960	.81	6.63	.04

Source: Morris A. Horowitz, "High Level Manpower in the Economic Development of Argentina," and William F. Whyte, "High Level Manpower
for Peru," in Frederick Harbison and Charles A. Myers, eds., *Manpower
and Education: Country Studies in Economic Development* (New York:
McGraw-Hill, 1965), pp. 53, 60.

demic work in the humanities and traditional professions is, in some areas, becoming less true. University academic life is decreasingly defined merely in terms of a few fixed, instructor-owned courses of study. Students are drawn increasingly from a wider range of social strata. University faculties in the professions, social sciences, and applied sciences have, in some universities, updated their offerings to make room for specializations demanded in industrialized societies. Research in the physical and social sciences, virtually unknown prior to World War II, has occasionally received attention by university authorities in recent years.

Data are available to indicate a slight shift in the professional goals of some Latin American university students in favor of engineering and commercial subjects. As Table V–5 indicates, Argentina and Peru may be taken as cases in point. In these nations, a trend away from the traditionally prestigious field of medicine may also be noticed. The situation with respect to law appears ambivalent and perhaps reflects national differences in the strength of educational traditions.

Summary

In viewing the educational problems of Latin America and the progress made toward creating educational systems that support development goals, perhaps four major points should be made. First, although resistance to change may be found among certain elite groups, national governments and national leaders generally are committed to economic development and subscribe to plans designed to raise the people's standard of living. Indeed, national development planning and educational planning are extremely popular concepts in Latin America. Unfortunately, much of the planning frequently becomes a paper exercise conducted in the isolated government offices of the capital city. These plans, conceived in the labyrinths of bureaucracy, frequently remain undefined in terms of the human talents, costs, and administrative machinery necessary for implementation.

Second, only slow progress is being made in achieving the goal of wide dissemination of educational opportunities among all areas and social and ethnic groupings. Throughout Latin America, illiteracy is very low among "whites," or *criollos*, but typically high among *mestizos* and *cholos* and extremely high among Indians. Indeed, as one author points out, "It is the established practice of the census officers in many of the countries to employ literacy as a major criterion in determining whether to classify persons as 'whites,' mestizos or Indians."[21] Moreover, most data indicate that among Latin American nations a very strong relationship persists between the percentage of literate people and the percentage of the population in urban areas.

Third, the educational systems have not fully responded to the impact of economic development and advances in science and technology. Latin American universities, for example, have not created a scientific or technological community. Secondary and higher education have not been sufficiently responsive to manpower needs. Nor has the variety of specialized institutions been created between the secondary schools and the universities, to provide for the contemporary technical needs of society and to offer educational options for the graduates of secondary education.

Fourth, in spite of the many problems and shortcomings in terms of economic development and educational progress, Latin America is relatively well off among the underdeveloped nations. Its top-level expertise rates well by worldwide standards. However, this progress is centered in "islands" of highly advanced economic and educational development throughout the region. The question remains, of course, as to how much drag will continue to be exercised by comfortable, traditional, elite groups, political instability, and culturally-isolated ethnic groups.

Suggested Readings for Chapter V

ADAMS, RICHARD N., *et al.* *Social Change in Latin America Today.* New York: Harper, Council on Foreign Relations, 1960.

BENJAMIN, HAROLD R. W. *Higher Education in the American Republics.* New York: McGraw-Hill, 1965.

[21] George Blanksten, "The Politics of Latin America," in Gabriel A. Almond and James S. Coleman, eds., *The Politics of the Developing Areas* (Princeton: Princeton University Press, 1960), p. 462.

74197

ECHAVARRIA, J. M., and BENJAMIN HIGGINS. *Social Aspects of Economic Development in Latin America II.* Paris: UNESCO, 1963.

"Education and Social Change in Latin America," *Rural Sociology*, Vol. 25, No. 1 (March 1960): MOREIRA, J. ROBERTO, "Rural Education and Socio-Economic Development in Brazil." BLAIR, THOMAS LUCIEN, "Social Structure and Information Exposure in Rural Brazil."

GOLDRICH, DANIEL. "Peasants' Sons in City Schools: An Inquiry into the Politics of Urbanization in Panama and Costa Rica," *Human Organization,* Vol. 23 (Winter 1964).

HAUSER, PHILIP M., ed. *Urbanization in Latin America.* Liege: UNESCO, 1961.

HAVIGHURST, ROBERT J., and ROBERTO MOREIRA. *Society and Education in Brazil.* Pittsburgh: University of Pittsburgh Press, 1965.

NASH, MANNING, "The Role of Village Schools in the Process of Cultural and Economic Modernization," *Social and Economic Studies*, Vol. 14, No. 1 (March 1965).

ROGERS, EVERETT M., and WILLIAM HERZOG. "Functional Literacy among Colombian Peasants," *Economic Development and Cultural Change*, Vol. 14, No. 2 (June 1966).

SILVERT, KALMAN H., and FRANK BONILLA. *Education and the Social Meaning of Development.* New York: American Universities Field Staff, 1961.

UNESCO, *América Latina. Proyecto Principal de Educación.* Boletín Trimestral, No. 14 (April–June 1962).

————. *Problems and Strategies of Educational Planning.* Paris: UNESCO, International Institute for Educational Planning, 1965.

————. *La Situación Educativa en América Latina: La Ensenanza Primaria: Estados, Problemas, Perspectivas.* New York: UNESCO, 1960.

WHITEFIELD, ANDREW. *Two Cities of Latin America.* Garden City, N.Y.: Doubleday, 1964.

WOLF, ERIC. "Types of Latin American Peasantry: A Preliminary Discussion," *American Anthropologist*, Vol. 57, No. 3 (1955), pp. 452–471.

CHAPTER VI

Some Common Educational Problems
in the Developing Nations

Middle Africa, South Asia, and Latin America share with one another, and with the developing nations in general, certain educational problems and aspirations. They have a common faith that education can contribute to their goals of economic growth, their nationhood, and the enhancement of human dignity. The developing nations wish to bolster their status in the world community, strengthen national cohesion, eradicate neocolonialism, spread "modern" attitudes, and maintain the fervor of their elites for national development. To these ends they have sought first to expand formal education at all levels to increasing numbers of people. Whatever the judgments against the allocation of scarce resources to certain levels and types of education, the political and ideological forces in favor of such extension are overwhelming.

In addition to expansion of enrollments, the developing nations are seeking to modify their educational systems to make them more efficient instruments in the achievement of national goals. Consideration is being given to new curricula, new instructional techniques, and to the provision of new linkages between education and other institutions. Educational planning in one form or another is seen as the means for fitting these changes into an educational policy that is progressive but not unduly disruptive.

It is the aim of this chapter to elaborate on the major problems manifest in the areas already discussed, and in developing countries generally. Some of the varying opinions and analyses of these problems are included in order to clarify possible solutions in the future. Some of the difficulties can be discussed under the following headings: (1) shortage of qualified teachers; (2) pupil dropouts or "wastage"; (3) inappropriate nature of curricula; (4) imbalance between rural and urban advancement; (5) inability to overcome traditions that inhibit female participation in education; (6) monopolization of higher-level graduates by government bureaucracies and the professions; and (7) lingering conservatism in the values found in educational systems.

Shortage of Qualified Teachers

Many of the underdeveloped countries are so short of people with enough education to make competent teachers that those who have their degree in education automatically become part of the intellectual elite, and move into non-teaching positions with high pay and prestige. Usually, scholarships for higher education, either at home or abroad, can be acquired for those who successfully complete secondary school, thus moving many potential teachers into a stream of experience that makes teaching an unlikely career choice. These observations are particularly true of secondary teaching.

As for primary teaching, the practice of using as teachers people who have had no more than a few years of primary schooling themselves is widespread. Their competence is therefore limited. They can hold classes, pass on some simple religious or traditional beliefs, and teach a limited reading vocabulary, but that is about all.

Since many underdeveloped countries are committed to educational expansion, they must attempt to get teachers from the more advanced countries. Although this runs against the nationalistic grain, it appears the only way out. The rather surprising high acceptance (at least temporarily) of "peace corps"-type teachers in many countries is a sign of this impasse. Still, the "foreignness" of education imparted by teachers from the advanced countries is disliked, and the goal is to supplant these people with indigenous teachers as quickly as possible. In a perceptive article, Becker points out the dilemma of educational administrators in underdeveloped countries who dislike the disrupting effects of Western knowledge, but at the same time realize that teaching the indigenous culture will not serve the national ends they have in mind. The wider community faces the same dilemma:

> The subordinate group [the mass of the people] may take one of several attitudes towards this question. They may desire strongly education in the culture of the dominant group because of the status advantages with which they know it can equip them. As in Ireland, and more recently, Africa, they may be caught up in a developing nationalism and wish to reject the dominant culture, uniting the institution of the school with their own language and culture.[1]

Whatever the wish of the elite or the masses, the need to utilize both underqualified teachers and expatriates is bound to exist for a rather long time in many underdeveloped countries. The expansion of the educational system may outstrip expansion in the economy, as in Korea, Taiwan, and the Philippines, and there may come a time when the government posts and higher professions are much more difficult to attain. However, this may not mean any great increase in available teachers, because the status, pay, and location of teaching jobs will often not be attractive enough to secondary graduates to induce them to give up hopes of gaining elite positions in the end.

A further word of caution should be introduced. Educators tend to assume that improving teachers will improve teaching, and conversely that instruction can be improved only by better teachers. In the light of advances in educational technology, this view should be examined critically. Certainly, educating better teachers must always remain an important educational goal; but in the absence of professional, self-directed teachers, such aids as nationally-prepared syllabi, laboratory materials, and programmed lessons can significantly improve instruction.

Failure of Schools to Hold Students

Obviously, elementary schools are less effective in supporting the development impulse if their impact is not sustained over a

[1] Howard S. Becker, "Schools and Systems of Social Status," *Phylon*, Vol. 6, No. 2 (1955), p. 163.

reasonable period of time. The ideal of schooling is initially difficult to instill, and many factors work against it. The child may be an economic asset to parents, and school may seem a threat to the realization of this asset; or parents may fear that new knowledge and ideas may alienate the child from traditional family ways. Yet, a change in attitude is necessary. To be effective, formal schooling must be conceived of as a legitimate part of the institutional structure. This transformation can be accelerated by propaganda, law, and economic arrangements.

Harbison and Myers note that in the least developed countries the holding power of schools is almost negligible:

> Many pupils start in the first grade, then drop out, and then come back again as repeaters and drop out again. Some schools in rural areas offer only one or two primary grades, because of lack of teachers capable of teaching the upper grades. In most schools, the teaching fails to interest or inspire the pupils.... The great majority of those who attend barely learn to read and write, and most of them lapse again into illiteracy after a few years.[2]

Even for those who stay, there is a tendency for the school to make each year a repetition of the last in order to overcome the general conditions in the cultural milieu that do not reinforce the learning experience.

The success of Japan in holding students, and creating meaningful literacy for nearly everyone within a half-century after the beginning of development, illustrates that lack of holding power can be overcome. But Japan had leadership that was willing to support schools by constant propaganda, legal enactments, and economic inducements. Also, the Japanese population had a spirit of disciplined national cohesion and some tradition of schooling even at the village level—characteristics absent in many of the presently underdeveloped countries.

To be effective, schools must be attended regularly and willingly; ideally, they should become associated with pleasure and profit, conditions not prevalent enough as yet in many poor countries. Therefore, to integrate schools in all kinds of social

[2] Frederick H. Harbison and Charles A. Myers, *Education, Manpower, and Economic Growth* (New York: McGraw-Hill, 1964), p. 54.

activities would be of practical value. Schools may become more appealing by providing obvious rewards for attendance, such as free meals. The potential profitability of schooling may be conveyed to students—and parents—by showing how education may increase vocational opportunities, incomes, standards of living, and the level of community life. For some students, the promise of a better understanding of the outside world and man's position in it may serve as a sufficient reward for schooling.

Inappropriate Nature of Curricula

The basic curricula issues at the pre-university level revolve around the extent of cultural adjustment, localization, and vocationalization. To what degree should the school use local materials of instruction, focus on local problems, develop local standards of performance? Should the school be primarily oriented to the nation, or to the world—and to what extent to technical and manpower needs or traditional university requirements?

The educational problem in terms of traditional curricula in the former British and French colonies was characterized in this passage from Balogh:

> In both the formerly English, and in the formerly French territories, a disdain of technical education has grown up . . . which has been exacerbated by the relating [sic] lowly status of technical schools and the restricted career possibilities open to their pupils. So long as the Civil Service and those appointments which are controlled or influenced by it . . . are the preserve of the non-technically educated, the best ability will obviously be directed into non-technical education. This will both justify and increase the initial disdain, and render economic and social progress more difficult.[3]

This quotation represents one point of view. However, the appropriate role of vocational education is perhaps the most controversial of all the curriculum issues. The argument for extensive vocational education runs as follows: Since 70 to 90 per cent of the people of the underdeveloped world are dependent

[3] T. Balogh, "Education and Economic Growth," *Kyklos*, Vol. 15, Fasc. 2 (1964), p. 270.

on agriculture, the need is for large-scale vocational programs at all educational levels, including an adequate emphasis on agricultural skills. It may then be argued that (1) schooling does not include enough skill courses; (2) the present schools are detrimental to progress because the graduates are not trained in vocations; and (3) academic and bookish education produces white-collar attitudes. However, there is increasing sentiment that this is a false argument. In the first place, observers point out that the need for agricultural and industrial development does not demand specific vocational programs in the lower schools. Second, general education and vocational education are not substitutes for each other, and much of what general education gives is crucial to development. Third, unemployment is due to lack of job opportunities, and expanding vocational school enrollments will not eliminate this problem. Such observers would further argue that general education should be emphasized at the pre-university level and that public and private firms should establish training programs for their personnel.

Perhaps the key to the curriculum controversy is secondary education. The issue should not be whether or not to have vocational education. Rather, the problem faced in most developing regions, but most dramatically in those South Asian and Latin American nations with unemployed secondary-school dropouts, is how to broaden the concept of secondary education in order to make it an outlet into industry and agriculture as well as into the university. Usually this will not mean substitution of "vocational" for "academic" courses, but the introduction of pre-vocational skills, attitudes, and concepts.

The problem, then, is not only disdain on the part of students for vocational education, as has sometimes been argued, but rather the whole "gestalt" of sentiments and action that makes the curricula dysfunctional for development. The basic need is to find a pattern of education that incorporates new knowledge and can be effectively extended to more and more people. Such schooling must bear at least a minimal relation to the daily life of the majority of the people if for no other reason than that learning by rote of seemingly meaningless materials is effective only among those who have an inordinately strong desire to use education as a way up the structural ladder.

Perhaps one of the most significant elements in curriculum reform is to strike a proper balance between local and national emphasis. The presentation of "local" information catches the interest of students; however, the creation of a national outlook requires the introduction of "national" material. Perhaps the strongest case for the use of local materials can be made in primary grades, where the geography of the region, examples in arithmetic, items for science lessons, and folktales can be used to enrich the curriculum and give meaning to otherwise abstract or incomprehensible information. Secondary schools must adopt a progressively larger amount of science; and any vocational education offered must concentrate on techniques not traditionally practiced. In science, local materials and applications can be employed generously, but the essential attitudes that are instilled should not be focused merely on local life. In universities the proportion of non-local material must, of course, be vastly increased. But some university students should be trained to become scholars concerned with local folklore and history, national history, archaeology, and linguistics.

The Imbalance between Rural and Urban Advancement

In most of the underdeveloped world there is a wide gulf between the amenities, wealth, excitement, and range of opportunities in the few relatively large urban centers and the much more backward rural or tribal areas. Contrasts between the modern buildings, boulevards, transportation, and cultural activities of the major city (usually the capital) and the countryside are striking to travelers who visit the less developed countries. The city is the home of those who largely control educational policy and, not unnaturally, the tendency is strong to use resources to expand education in the showplace of the nation. The secondary-school graduates, and often primary-school graduates as well, migrate to the city with hopes of job placement or further education. Since urbanization and educational level are positively correlated,

and since educated persons constitute a group for whom formal
education has a secure place in their cultural values, pressure is
continually exerted for the allocation of resources to education
in the main cities of the country.

The difference between educational opportunities in the rural
and urban areas is very evident. Urban inhabitants (or even
inhabitants of large towns) have a much greater chance of entering the higher levels of schooling that do rural people. In Ghana,
for example, the population in cities of over 50,000 had fourteen
times more chance of entering the fifth form of secondary education than did the people in villages of under 5,000.[4]

In the developed nations, conscious policy or fortuitous circumstances at one point or another have acted to redress the
imbalance between urban and rural educational development. In
the United States, the political power of rural groups was greater
in state and national governments than their relative numbers
might indicate; consequently, resources for education were pulled
from city areas to rural areas by legislated formulas. Furthermore, the land-grant colleges provided opportunities for children
from rural areas to go on to higher schooling at low cost, and
developed an approach to instruction that combined general education with practical learning in agricultural and other pursuits.
Japan, following the American pattern, made agricultural courses
available to rural-oriented students in higher schools before 1900.
The number of students enrolled in agricultural courses in higher
education grew from 15 in 1875 to 986 in 1890, and 2,172 in
1910.[5]

In Russia, the expansion of schools into largely rural eastern
areas was one of the important accomplishments of the 1920's
and 1930's. In 1917, educational enrollment ratios of elementary-
school-age children had already reached well over 40 per cent in
and around the great cities of St. Petersburg, Moscow, Kiev,

<hr />

[4] R. Clignet, "The Legacy in West African Educational Systems: Its Meaning
and Ambiguities," *Comparative Education Review*, Vol. XII, No. 1 (February
1968), pp. 57–67.

[5] Ministry of Education, Government of Japan, *Japan's Growth and Education*
(Tokyo: 1963), p. 168.

Odessa, Minsk, and Kharkov. However, at this time among the Uzbeks, for example, there was only about 2 per cent literacy and about a 2 per cent enrollment ratio for elementary-school-age children. One of the most significant of all Communist party goals, and one largely fulfilled, has been the implantation of elementary education in vast rural areas that had had little contact with education prior to the Revolution.

The most obvious way to begin to solve the problem of rural-urban imbalance in educational development is through concerted determination on the part of the leadership to propagandize and enforce a great effort to expand rural facilities. Most of the underdeveloped countries cannot depend on the fortunate combination of events that favored rural education in the United States during its various periods of development. It may prove very difficult to combine a relatively democratic political order with vigorous action to redress the urban-rural imbalance in education.

Problem of Female Participation in Educational Development

One of the most persistent obstacles to an adequate development role for education is the tendency in many countries for cultural beliefs to stand in the way of rapid extension of education to women. The belief is widespread that woman's place is in the home and that formal education is unlikely to aid in fulfilling this basic role. In fact, it is often feared that education of women will weaken the family, rearrange the hierarchy in the family and village, and work against religion. All these fears have a ring of truth. Development does demand an altered family structure, a different use of many women's time, and more, not less, use of achievement rather than sex ascription for status placement. Ashley Montagu described the almost universal tendency of undeveloped, nonliterate peoples to view women as inherently inferior:

> In all non-literate societies the roles of the sexes are distinguished, and it is doubtful whether there are any in which women are not regarded as inferior to men, and this is in matrilineal as well as in patrilineal societies. It is extremely rare for women to be admitted to the council of elders, and women are practically every-

where excluded from mysteries and professions which are the pre-
rogatives of men. Even cannibalistic activities are restricted to
men, and women are usually deprived of participation in such deli-
cate activities.[6]

The feeling that education is not for girls is particularly strong
in Moslem countries. For example, in the region of Bahawalpur,
W. Pakistan, there were in the late 1950's 17,000 students in
grant-receiving schools; only 750 of these were girls (about 4 per
cent).[7] A high degree of discrimination toward girls is found in
all underdeveloped countries, and even in the developed ones
there remain perhaps an irreducible minimum of status ascription
by sex and some clear educational and professional disabilities for
women and girls.

Japan, again, is an example of a country that greatly reduced
educational disadvantages for women in a very short time.   In
1875, 18.6 per cent of the female population of elementary school
age attended school; in 1900 this ratio exceeded 90 per cent.[8]   In
schools above the elementary level female attendance grew rapidly during this period, although at a slower rate than male.

In one sense, the education of women is the most crucial factor
in educational development. The greatest barrier to development
is the persistence of unspecialized institutional structures. When
too many functions are tied to one institutional complex, the
difficulty of altering the patterns of social interaction is tremen-
dously heightened. Some have argued that the hold of a multifunctional religious institution must be modified, and some have
seen monolithic kinship structures as the main obstacle. In fact,
functions must be taken from both church and family if the development of a society is to maintain momentum. But as long as
half the population (the female) is kept tied to traditional values,
is given no hint of alternative behavior patterns, and is set in rigid
ascribed statuses, the development process faces strong forces
that can slow or reverse its progression.

[6]Ashley Montagu, *Anthropology and Human Nature* (Boston: Porter Sargent,
1957), p. 65.
[7]Freeland Abbot, "The Makatab of Bahawalpur," *Saturday Review*, Vol. 44
(July 15, 1961), p. 64.
[8]Ministry of Education, *op. cit.*, p. 42.

In one key area alone the lack of education among women is particularly harmful. Most observers agree that some form of controlling the population explosion in developing countries is requisite to their further development. Although there are primitive people who have devised methods of birth limitation, habits of contraception are likely to grow slowly in an illiterate, or partly literate, female population. But in village and peasant cultures, where the gap in status between men and women often widens and the hold of a more elaborate institutionalized religion is strengthened, the chances of significantly reducing average live births per woman is almost hopeless, unless the progress of female education at least roughly matches that of the male.

The Monopolization of Higher Graduates by Government and the Higher Professions

Although an educated leadership in government is crucial, it cannot be sustained unless people with attitudes and training in sympathy with development become widely dispersed throughout the occupational structure. In developed countries, through chance or policy, large numbers of graduates of higher schooling found their way, rather soon after development began, into industrial management, agricultural endeavors, teaching, communication, transportation, domestic arts, and technical fields. Japan had no engineering students in 1875, but had 3,769 in 1910 and 103,000 in 1960. Similar rapid growth in agricultural studies, education, science, economics, business, secondary technical, secondary fishery, and domestic arts occurred from 1880 on. The USSR, of course, provides an impressive example of a concerted effort to spread educated people rapidly throughout a great range of activities. Schwartz had this comment:

> In expanding its labor force during 1928–40, the Soviet regime had to contend with the problem of quality as well as quantity. The great majority of new workers recruited for nonagricultural employment during these years had never had any previous experience or familiarity with machines or their operation. They were not accustomed to the discipline required in a factory or on a railroad. At a higher level of competence, the newly expanded productive system required far larger numbers of engineers, chem-

ists, metallurgists, accountants, executives, and other directing personnel than had ever been required in the Soviet Union before.... The number of Soviet citizens studying in schools of all types, including extension-course students, reached 47.4 million in 1938–39, probably close to half the entire population if we exclude the aged and preschool children.... The frenzied educational drive of the 1930's, accompanied by the enormous increase in students and graduates, was quite naturally accompanied by an appreciable decline in the quality of training.... Under these conditions many skilled workers, technicians, and directing personnel had to finish their education on the job, a costly process.... Out of the confusion and frenzy of this period were born both the new labor force and the technical managerial force of the Soviet's economy, both of which have been developed greatly since the early years of the 1930's. Without the 1,500,000 specialists graduated by the Soviet secondary schools and higher education institutions, the realization of the country's industrialization would have been impossible.[9]

In many underdeveloped countries it is much too common for the great majority of secondary or university graduates to refuse employment except in public functionary jobs or higher professions such as law, university instruction, medicine, and sometimes the church. Of course, other employment opportunities may exist, but they may be remote from the largest city or at a lower level of prestige, or may seem to be only a somewhat elaborated semiskilled job. Moreover, alternative employment opportunities, as in the case of newer entrepreneurial pursuits and the applied sciences, may place the graduate in the uncomfortable vanguard working against traditional habits. For all these reasons, plus the willingness of too many governments to try and buy popularity by loading the bureaus with superfluous but politically-potent secondary and higher graduates, a great brake on development is created.

Lingering Conservatism in the Values Found in Educational Systems

The values that pervade many school situations in the developing nations are particularistic and traditional. A beginning must

[9] Harry Schwartz, *Russia's Soviet Economy* (New York: Prentice-Hall, 1950), pp. 444–445.

be made in modifying at least some of these values in order to make the school more of a force for modernization.

One of the most likely value orientations that can be reformed in the school setting is the much too prevalent fatalistic belief that events cannot be predicted or controlled. Schools can provide a social context in which individuals are able to predict the behavior of others, and circumstances in general. In this way, the concept of a more predictable social context and universe may be established. The regularity and lawfulness of natural phenomena (birds come from eggs, objects fall down, and so on) can be demonstrated in a convincing manner through science courses, laboratory experiments, and field trips. Finally, the scientific method, critical thinking, and the careful analysis and evaluation of empirical evidence may be taught in the higher grades.

The predictability of the social context and of men's actions can be demonstrated best, perhaps, by the operation of the school itself. If, for example, the rules of the school are reasonable, clearly stated, and always enforced—by punishment or reward for behavior—students can generalize from this social phenomenon to larger social units. But if the school operates haphazardly, and the staff allows or encourages favoritism, most students will regard this as just another example of the capriciousness of man and nature.

The possibility of equitable and regularized social relationships outside the school may be demonstrated initially by studying the behavior of men who perform roles in some established institutions. Later, students may be taught that individuals who do not live up to their institutional roles are punished, and that the fear of punishment and hope of reward serve to stabilize behavior patterns and make them predictable. The major problem, of course, is that too many social relationships in underdeveloped countries are, in fact, capricious and personal. The taking of bribes, the inequitable administration of justice, and the intermittent turmoil in political life are examples of phenomena that have to be satisfactorily explained to the student so as not to invalidate the principle of equity and predictability of human action.

The operation of the school should also be directed toward establishing an orientation toward the future. This, of course, involves the predictability and equity in the social phenomena mentioned above. The fact that school attendance, study, and hard work usually lead to graduation and upward occupational mobility demonstrates, within the school context, the efficacy of the long-range point of view. The rewards enjoyed by students in the upper grades who have successfully completed the hard work in lower grades are the source of the vicarious reinforcement in terms of which younger students act. Finally, successful graduates who have achieved high positions in the community exemplify the possibilities to be gained in working for future benefits. The possibility that the future can be, and likely will be, better than the past is an important lesson to convey. There must be a belief that education offers practical benefits in the future. The problem, in many countries, of an unemployed "intelligentsia" is doubly serious in that its existence not only saps the present but makes difficult the inculcation among the young of a belief in the future. Great care must be taken, therefore, to establish reasonable goals and to define rewards that can be attained.

Success in using education to establish new behavior patterns that support the development process will depend in large degree on the absence of conflicting demands that might reduce the student's rate of learning. It will be necessary, then, to neutralize as far as possible traditional influences exerted by the student's family, his companions, and his home community in general.

Schools extend the student's understanding and interest beyond the local scene, and emphasize new ideas, places, activities, and possibilities; this naturally reduces the importance of the past and the things and people associated with it. Furthermore, schools increase the choices open to students—in terms of jobs, friends, and interpretations of social and physical phenomena; consequently, old ways become less significant. The boarding school, by its very operation, greatly reduces the influences of the "home town" and the family. It is, of course, expensive and must be used selectively. Another way of decreasing the influence of the past is to expose the student to a variety of viewpoints by having children from various social classes, regions, and cultural backgrounds in the same class. Confronted by such heterogeneity, the individual's faith in the old ideas expressed by his family and home village is challenged, and often modified.

The reduction of parental and kin influence will increase the student's reliance on his teachers. Teachers, who often serve as models, should be selected with great care: if they are to serve as role models and as symbols of the world, they must be part of it. If primary education—the only educational level available to large numbers of people in most underdeveloped countries—is to support development by the modernization of attitudes, elementary teachers must share a considerable number of modern values and attitudes themselves. This factor should receive the highest priority in teacher selection and training. Teachers should identify and be familiar with the modern world. Of course, they also need some identification with and sensitivity to their students' cultural experiences and background. In one sense, teachers must be "marginal men" in order to bridge the gap between the traditional and modern sectors of the society. Tradition-bound teachers cannot have modern reference value for their pupils; on the other hand, students will fail to accept as models teachers with modern orientation who misunderstand, degrade, or insult them.

Summary

The variety of obstructions to using education more effectively in the development process is linked to the variety of social contexts in which the schools find themselves. Social conditions are influential in affecting the kind and extent of schooling and in raising or lowering wastage rates. Similarly, the lack of education for women, the occasional absence of demand for education, and the frustrating language problem common to developing areas have roots in the value structure and class and ethnic composition. Even the problem of quality of instruction is not solely a professional question, for parents who have received little formal education (as have the bulk of the populations in the developing nations) usually give only slight attention to quality, no matter how vociferous they may be in demanding more educational opportunities.

Although at one level of abstraction and generality, the problems and patterns of educational poverty are similar among developing nations, there are, as we have continually cautioned throughout the text, important nuances of difference. Middle Africa, for example, quantitatively and qualitatively has educational problems of the greatest intensity. On the other hand, African nations may experience less resistance to educational growth than either South Asia or Latin America, both of which have more strongly-entrenched elitist groups, some of whom fear a loss of status from extension of educational opportunity. All the developing nations have been drawn from Western education, culture, and manpower in moving along the path of development; yet all are now conscious of the need to break away from reliance on the West. Some, such as Communist China, attempt to violently reject Western ways and institutions, while others seek only to put their peculiar cultural stamp on them.

These problems place constraints on educational development, since the growth of an educational system is limited by the amount of societal support and the rate at which resources, teachers, and facilities can be developed. For example, an educational system, if expanding, makes heavy demands on the manpower supply. Moreover, the maintenance of internal consistency is an ever-present problem, for the growth at high educational levels is determined by the growth at lower levels (even higher quality of instruction at higher levels is to some extent dependent on the quality of teaching at lower levels). Finally, there is the constraint of financial resources. Although a high correlation exists between low rates of educational investment and low levels of economic development, there is, at present, no standard that can serve adequately as a guideline for the rate of investment in education. These constraints add to the significance of careful thought and planning for the total educational system on the part of the developing nations.

Suggested Readings for Chapter VI

ADAMS, DON, and JOSEPH P. FARRELL, eds. *Education and Social Development.* Syracuse: Syracuse University, Center for Development Education, 1966, mimeo.

BEEBY, C. E. *The Quality of Education in Developing Countries.* Cambridge: Harvard University Press, 1966.

CURLE, ADAM. *Educational Strategy for Developing Societies.* London: Tavistock Publications, 1963.

HANSON, JOHN W., and COLE S. BREMBECK, eds. *Education and the Development of Nations.* New York: Holt, Rinehart and Winston, 1966.

HARBISON, FREDERICK H., and CHARLES A. MYERS. *Education, Manpower, and Economic Growth.* New York: McGraw-Hill, 1964.

CHAPTER VII

Educational Planning for National Development

The developing nations of Africa, Asia, and Latin America have been described as "century-skippers"—a term referring more to their social and economic aspirations than to their successes in development. Implied is the notion that today's developing nations seek to achieve greater results in much shorter time than was required by the developed nations in their earlier stages of development. The instrument most relied on to promote rapid and equitable change is national planning. Thus a principle emerges in most of the developing nations that was largely absent in the earlier stages of Western development, namely, *that national government can and should assume extensive responsibilities for guiding the process of national development.*

This view of the necessity and efficacy of planning is increasingly reflected in those agencies of government that administer education. Nearly all of the Latin American, South Asian, and Middle African nations, for example, have, internally or with the support of outside assistance, engaged in some limited way in national educational planning. Moreover, international planning conferences have been held to consider regional educational targets and to analyze possibilities for international cooperation.

With so much attention being given to educational planning and so much hope being attached to it as a key process in maximizing education's role in development, it has been singled out in this final chapter for special emphasis. The concern here is not so much in reviewing the progress made in educational planning (some description of this is found in Chapters III, IV, and V) as in trying to clarify the meaning of the term, to ascertain the manner in which the goals and priorities in national educational plans may be derived, and, most importantly, to assess the prospects and limitations of national educational planning in the developing nations.

Defining Educational Planning

Throughout human history change has been relatively gradual and based on *chance discoveries* of solutions to practical problems of survival and organization. In the last few centuries change has increasingly become the result of conscious efforts to alter or "improve" a technique or institution. Attention to change was frequently limited to one sphere, with little effort exerted to anticipate resultant changes in related activities. Most recently, attempts have been made to obtain specific consequences or sequences of change through introducing appropriate innovations and anticipating the derivative consequences. These attempts to anticipate and influence consequences in change may be called *planning.*[1]

All or nearly all of the nations of the world are now committed to some degree to the "mechanism" of educational change called educational planning. Capitalistic democracies such as the United States may be somewhat self-conscious about the "socialist" implications of national planning in any field; yet at all levels of government the decisions for the allocation of resources are made "planfully" rather than on an *ad hoc* basis.

While the commitment to planning is extensive and the number of national educational plans produced in the last few years numerous, the planning process is rarely defined with precision. A definition developed at the Inter-American Seminar in 1958, and widely referred to in subsequent regional and international meetings, reads as follows:

> The overall planning of education is a continuous, systematic process, involving the application and coordination of social research methods, and of principles and techniques of education, administration, economics and finance, with participation and support of the general public, in private as well as State activities, with a view to securing adequate education for the people, with

[1] Don Adams and Joseph P. Farrell, eds., *Education and Social Development* (Syracuse: Syracuse University, Center for Development Education, 1966, mimeo) pp. 12–13. (Original statement by Professor Alvin Boskoff, Emory University.)

definite aim, and in well-defined stages, and to providing everyone
with an opportunity of developing his potentialities and making
the most effective contribution to the social, cultural and economic
development of the country.[2]

This is obviously meant to be a comprehensive, somewhat
idealized statement of educational planning, of value possibly as a
goal toward which planning efforts can be directed. There can be
little quarrel with the emphasis on planning as "a continuous,
systematic process" involving both pedagogical and social scientific insights. Yet, as has been pointed out, ".... one does wonder
just how men with all these assortments of knowledge (and the
'general public' thrown in) are to be integrated into a planning
team."[3]

Two further serious limitations of this definition may be noted.
First, no mention is made of the relation between educational
innovation and planning. Should a major purpose of educational
planning be to encourage educational innovation? Second, although it is suggested that educational planning must reflect and
coordinate the views of different disciplines, no rationale, or
theory incorporating these approaches in planning, is suggested.[4]

A simpler definition of educational planning, but one that still
has many of the shortcomings of the one above, is "the process of
preparing a set of decisions for future action pertaining to education."[5] A somewhat more complete definition might read: "Educational planning involves the application of a rational system of
choices among feasible courses of educational investment and
other development actions based on a consideration of economic
and social costs and benefits."[6]

As used in this chapter, educational planning will refer to the
process of making decisions regarding the educational system for

[2]Quoted in UNESCO, *Elements of Educational Planning* (Paris: The Organization, 1963), p. 13.
[3]C. Arnold Anderson and Mary Jean Bowman, "Theoretical Considerations
in Educational Planning," in Don Adams, ed., *Educational Planning* (Syracuse:
Syracuse University Press, 1964), p. 10.
[4]*Ibid.*, p. 11.
[5]Adapted from Y. Dror, "The Planning Process," *International Review of
Administrative Science,* Vol. 29, No. 1 (1963), p. 50.
[6]Adapted from Albert Waterston, "What Do We Know About Planning?"
International Development Review, Vol. 7 (December 1965).

the purpose of attuning the effort to the development goals of a nation. Thus conceived, it involves more than merely establishing on paper future educational targets or the administration of pre-scribed governmental funds for education. It is a process that becomes refined by analysis of the past and future, as well as the present.

Determining Goals and Targets

Educational planning might be considered either as a separate sector or as part of overall development planning. Our focus will be on the latter. Given our definition and focus, certain logical steps in the process may be identified:

1. A national development plan is formulated, based on the goals of the nation. For example, India, in its Third Five-Year Plan, states its development objective simply but vaguely as pro-viding "the masses of the Indian people the opportunity to lead a good life."[7] Pakistan has developed a series of long-range goals toward which its five-year plans aim. These involve:

(*a*) Quadrupling of the Gross National Product and doubling of the per capita income.

(*b*) Provision of full employment.

(*c*) Parity of per capita incomes between East and West Pakistan.

(*d*) Achievement of universal literacy.

(*e*) Elimination of dependence on foreign assistance.[8]

These goals are largely focused on economic growth and the equitable distribution of its benefits, and certain social targets (universal literacy). Similar goals would be formulated for most other developing nations. Usually the initial specific allocation of resources that is meant to implement the plan reflects a mixture of general priority decisions (whether to emphasize industry or agriculture, for example), arbitrary judgments, and a considerable amount of compromise on the part of the various government offices and ministries involved. If rationality enters into the

[7]*Third Five-Year-Plan* (Delhi: Government of India Press, 1961), p. 1.
[8]*Third Five-Year-Plan* (Karachi: Government of Pakistan, 1965), p. 17.

planning process, it is largely through analysis in the establishment of economic targets, and in the adjustments required in the
economic structure to meet the targets. Again using Pakistan for
illustrative purposes, the Third Five-Year Plan (1965–1969) calls
for a 6.5 per cent rate of growth of GNP. To achieve this target
an investment strategy is formulated, based on the analysis of past
rates of growth in the various sectors.

2. Educational planning, or planning for the allocation of resources to the educational sector, is thus linked first to the procedures used in general development planning. If the goals and
targets are the results or partially the result of economic analysis,
the educational plan should reflect this analysis. From whatever
evidence is available, adjustments must be made in the educational enrollments and curricula in order to maximize the economic contribution of the educational system. The goal of
integration between educational and overall development planning is illustrated by the Soviet case:

> Every development plan (long-term, medium-term, short-term)
> contains targets for education and culture and provisions for ap-
> propriate financial outlays. These educational targets are closely
> linked with the other economic and social targets. The thinking
> behind this is that there is no point in creating new productive ca-
> pacities if there are not enough engineers and qualified workers to
> operate them. There is little sense either in turning out skills for
> which no productive employment is in sight. The two processes
> must be co-related so as to avoid waste of resources, both material
> and human, and maximize the rate of growth.[9]

If, on the other hand, the overall development plan reflects only
the more general cultural, economic, and political goals of a nation and an essentially arbitrary allocation of resources, educational planning has little to draw upon in establishing specific
targets. That is, the planning process still attempts to maximize
the contribution of the educational system to development goals,
but, lacking a specific reference point, must rely on general insights into linkages between education and social and economic
change.

[9] Raymond Lyons, ed., *Problems and Strategies of Educational Planning* (Paris:
UNESCO, 1965), p. 98.

In practice, the most common approach by nations to educational planning is what has sometimes been termed the "social method."[10] Educational needs are viewed in terms of certain general cultural and political objectives, such as a certain level of literacy, and universal primary education, with no precise assessment of the social or economic contributions of the schools attempted. This approach takes into account the current demand for education and may make future projections of demand by considering anticipated population changes, and changes in national goals. If they are to be implemented, plans arrived at in this manner are subsequently modified in keeping with available finances.

Most regional conferences (some of which were commented on in Chapter II), such as those held in Addis Ababa, Karachi, and Bogotá, use the "social method" to identify long-range educational targets. The goals of universal primary education for Africa (1980) and Asia (1970), for example, are not based on an analysis of the impact of primary-school graduates on the rate of economic growth. Nor are such goals based in any measurable way on the contribution of primary schooling to citizenship or any of the noneconomic aspects of the good life. Rather, with some knowledge of the needs of development, some insight into the factors that accelerate and inhibit educational expansion, and a strong commitment to education as a human right, a consensus is reached on reasonable expectations.

If the national development plan lays heavy stress on economic development, attempts may be made to link the educational system to economic goals through the manpower approach. In essence, this involves estimating the necessary additions of personnel with various occupational skills to the labor force during the planning period and deciding, for each occupational category, what the appropriate educational qualifications are.[11] The as-

[10]It has been said with regard to Latin American nations, for example, that although many plans exist, "There is no case where an educational plan has been interpreted at the financial and manpower levels with a general development plan." Maximo Halty Carrere, "Some Aspects of Educational Planning in Latin America," *Problems and Strategies of Educational Planning* (Paris: UNESCO, 1965), p. 54.

[11]Herbert S. Parnes, "Assigning the Educational Needs of a Nation," in Adams, *op. cit.*, p. 55.

sumption is that the educational system's first task is to provide the skills and knowledge required to perform the work needed for national production.[12] Here, of course, is where much controversy lies. Programs of "practical" and vocational education frequently appear to offer the most direct linkages, yet recent experiences have made us wary of the obvious. First, the school is not the only agency that produces occupational skills. Extension education, on-the-job training in industrial concerns, apprenticeship programs, and other arrangements provide out-of-school skill training.

Second, it must not be concluded that only vocational schools have an economic return on their investment. Indeed, one of the striking areas of educational failure in the underdeveloped countries has been vocational education, particularly at the primary and secondary-school levels. Many national leaders, seeing the paucity of industrial, commercial, and agricultural skills among the population, have looked to vocational schools to meet these shortages—a view that frequently has been reinforced by the thinking of American technical-assistance advisers. Exceeding faith in the economic contribution of vocational schools is unfounded for two reasons. Vocational schools can attract students only if the incentives they offer or the rewards they promise are sufficiently attractive. As long as the academic schools are the path to the universities and to prestige positions, good students are not likely to choose vocational education. Frequently those who do enroll in a vocational school will try to pressure the institution into becoming a second-rate academic school whose major purpose is university preparation. Moreover, graduates of vocational schools frequently ignore their training and seek nontechnical pursuits. Rejection of vocational schooling by many youths in the developing areas does not necessarily reflect "only wanting white-collar work" or being "unwilling to get hands dirty," for it may be a most realistic appraisal of the comparative rewards of vocational and academic schooling.

[12] Students interested in further study of the manpower approach might see Frederick H. Harbison and Charles A. Myers, *Education, Manpower, and Economic Growth* (New York: McGraw-Hill, 1964), Chapter 9, and Herbert S. Parnes, *Forecasting Educational Needs for Economic and Social Development* (Paris: OECD, 1962).

Another important consideration must be the comparative expense of preparing skilled manpower through schools and job-related training. Without arguing that vocational schools have no useful function to perform, it should be pointed out that they are very expensive. Hundreds of thousands of dollars of American technical-assistance money have been spent in underdeveloped areas on elaborate vocational facilities that have rarely, if ever, been used efficiently. On the other hand, some vocational schools have had a very direct impact over a period of years on the productive output of a nation. Partly it is a question of planning and a realistic perception of conditions. With sufficient incentives, a surplus of graduates of academic secondary schools, and employment opportunities for vocational graduates available, vocational schools may function well. In any case, as a vital adjunct to the regular school system, the full potential of the ongoing governmental and private organizations for skill training needs to be explored constantly.

Disregarding, for the moment, the dangers of equating manpower needs with vocational training, and without going into the technical methods of estimating future manpower requirements, it is clear that the manpower approach could indicate to the educational planner valuable information on the enrollments and graduates from various levels and types of schooling needed. In outline form, the procedures for translating manpower requirements into enrollments might be as follows:

1. Preparation of an inventory of manpower for the current year, differentiating between the employed and the unemployed, and cross-classifying the labor force by occupation and industry, by occupation and education, and by educational attainment and age.

2. Estimation of the size of the labor force for the forecast year.

3. Estimation of total employment in each sector and branch of the economy for the forecast year—for example, agriculture, mining, textile manufacturing, metal products, trade, and transportation.

4. Conversion of the data on requirements by occupational category into data on requirements by educational qualifications.

5. Comparison of the projected structure of the labor force by educational qualification with the existing structure.

6. Calculation of replacement needs in each educational category resulting from deaths, retirements, net emigration, and withdrawal from the labor force.

7. Adjustment for attrition rates and calculation of the enrollments required.

8. On the basis of required enrollments, calculation of needs for additional teachers and facilities.[13]

Criticism of the Social and Manpower Approaches

If need has meaning only in relation to objectives, as distinct from wishes or desires, the problem with the so-called social approach is that need is not really ascertained. Moreover, there is a circularity to the argument for using demand for schooling to calculate "needs" for education. The number of youths who seek education beyond the compulsory stage is at least partly dependent on costs and inducements—matters to a degree controllable by government policy. Thus "Society's needs determine policy which conditions demand for [school] places."[14]

On the other hand, social demand is a very real factor in educational planning. If there is strong pressure among the population for a certain amount or kind of schooling, such pressure constitutes a political if not a developmental need. What political leaders can resist the demand for primary schooling that is sweeping many of the underdeveloped nations? Or the national pressure for prestige-giving universities? When the desire for education is the development goal (as it may well be among traditional social groups and in the less familiar trades and professions), a consideration of demand is also essential to educational planning. In this case, the goal of the national leaders must be to raise the demand to the necessary level. Thus, considerable attention in Middle Africa is being given to the resistance to schooling by certain tribal groups, and in Latin America to the "Indian problem." Plan formulation must reflect such conditions, and plan

[13] Harbison and Myers, *op. cit.*, pp. 55–56.
[14] *Ibid.*

implementation must be linked with innovative efforts to increase responsiveness to educational goals. Thus, school building programs in rural areas may need to be linked with, or even follow, community development attempts. And a certain level of efficiency is required in the infrastructure of transportation and communication to transmit, reinforce, and coordinate any national plans for educational change.

The terms "social justice" and "social democratization" are sometimes associated with the social approach. The phrase "equality of educational opportunity" expresses much of the meaning of these terms. Although development, structurally defined, would not appear to presuppose educational equality of opportunity, this social goal is a real part of the planning scene. Since it is real, the meaning, or rather, meanings, of the phrase "equality of educational opportunity" need to be considered. The concept of equity as applied to education might mean (*a*) schooling sufficient to bring every child to a given standard; (*b*) education sufficient to permit each person to reach his own potential; (*c*) continued opportunities for schooling so long as gains in learning per input of teaching match some agreed norm.[15]

Not only would the different interpretations attached to equality suggest different educational policies, but not all (certainly not the first two) of the interpretations support policies of efficiency. "... equity is a goal or end in each of its variants, efficiency is a rationality concept: to get the most out of the least, whatever the nature of the rewards or ends may be."[16] Thus, while the goal of equality of opportunity suggests that the disadvantaged population groups should receive special assistance, the goal of efficiency might well support maximum encouragement for groups demonstrating the largest capacity for education. Even the proponents of the manpower approach to educational planning do not usually advocate limiting educational policies to those that are designed to produce sufficient manpower. Moreover, most governments either make explicit manpower forecasts or have formed some "opinion" as to manpower needs. Thus, analyses of man-

---

[15]Anderson and Bowman, *op. cit.*, p. 15.
[16]*Ibid.*, p. 16.

power needs to some extent may be seen as adding rationality to procedures already in effect. The question becomes not whether forecasts are to be made, but the extent to which they are going to be as systematic as possible, based on all the evidence that can be marshaled.[17]

There are two types of criticism of the manpower approach, both of which merit serious consideration. First, to some educators, it borders on the immoral to examine the educational system basically as a means for occupational training. Indeed, some find the language of economic analysts in terms of "inputs," "outputs," and "productivity of the schools," insulting when applied to institutions bearing a significant brunt of the tasks of socialization and transmitting the cultural heritage. Sometimes a question has been raised regarding the possibility of assessing formal education in terms of criteria drawn from the outside. An extension of this view, which is not necessarily encumbered by the romantic notions frequently attributed to educators, is the argument that society's needs cannot be equated with occupational needs. Even if the training of manpower is accepted as one function of the schools, it does not follow that schools should be the only or the prime source of skilled manpower.

A second category of criticism is more technical in nature. In spite of the conceptual neatness that, at least theoretically, allows a precise equivalence of formal schooling and developmental needs for skills, skepticism has been voiced in many quarters as to the accuracy of long-term manpower forecasting. While planning, in terms of facilities and personnel needed to train new manpower groups, requires ten to twenty years' lead time, manpower forecasting has demonstrated reasonable accuracy only on a much shorter basis.

At least two reasons for the inaccuracy can be noted. First, at certain levels of skills and specialization, a considerable amount of "substitutability" is possible. That is, many occupations do not require extensive amounts of unique vocational education. For example, there is a high degree of substitution between ad-

[17] Herbert S. Parnes, "Manpower Analysis in Educational Planning," in H. S. Parnes, ed., *Planning Education for Economic and Social Development* (Paris: OECD, 1963), p. 76.

ministrative positions requiring advanced levels of education. Moreover, the preferred educational level of occupations changes; e.g., in the United States, in 1966, there were higher educational demands for skilled labor than in 1900.

Manpower planning has been carried out most extensively in the industrially advanced nations. For a host of reasons, including lack of needed labor-force data, the problems of forecasting are greatest in the underdeveloped nations. Moreover, as Cash has indicated, there are several highly questionable assumptions, at least when the manpower planning model is applied to Africa.[18] To use but one illustration, Cash questions whether the high geographic and occupational mobility of labor assumed in manpower planning can be realized in societies where movement is strongly affected by social obligation and affiliation.[19]

The basic question, however, does not concern the presence of shortcomings in the manpower approach. Instead, one must consider whether or not the manpower approach can make a positive contribution to educational planning. Are manpower analyses and forecasting worth the effort? A qualified *yes* may be given. At least, as a crude guide, the manpower approach can make a contribution to educational planning. For example, it would be useful to differentiate between occupations requiring different levels of education; and between those requiring scientific-technical training and those requiring a general education (as did the manpower surveys on East Africa referred to in Chapter III). However, it does seem highly questionable that sophisticated and intricate manpower forecasts are possible in most underdeveloped nations. Such forecasts, considering all the uncertainties involved, and the heavy reliance on individual judgment in lieu of adequate data, may actually be more harmful than beneficial to educational planning.

Obstacles to Precision in Assessing Educational Needs

The problem with regard to more precise assessment of educational needs can be traced to our lack of understanding of the

[18] Webster C. Cash, "A Critique of Manpower and Educational Change in Africa," *Economic Development and Cultural Change*, Vol. 14 (October 1965).

[19] *Ibid.*, p. 38.

development process in general, and the educative process in
particular. Curle, for example, who has been intimately ac-
quainted with more than a decade's national planning efforts in
Pakistan, points out:

> It is interesting that the broad lines of educational policy and the
> financial allocations for education, in all three plans with which I
> have been associated, were arrived at in a very arbitrary way. No-
> body had, and so far as I know nobody has, any reliable empirical
> method of determining the appropriate proportion of planned ex-
> penditure to be devoted to education, or social welfare, or health,
> or any of the factors which do not give a directly measurable
> return.[20]

The problem in judging education's peculiar contribution to
development is the fact that the effects of schooling are all inter-
woven with other social influences on behavior. That is, it is very
difficult to ascertain the difference between education as a necessary but not sufficient condition and education as a necessary and
sufficient condition. Also, knowledge, skills, and attitudes are
acquired in a variety of in-school and out-of-school contexts, and
the presence of an educated population does not always accelerate
the development process. As a number of economists have observed, steel mills and large manufacturing plants do not suddenly
rise because there are skilled people available to operate them.

Much has been written differentiating the economic from other
goals of development. This separation is recognized as analytical,
but it is of value in facilitating the use of different scholarly methods of inquiry. As has been argued, noneconomic factors, such
as social structure, political organizations, and individual attitudes and values influence economic growth and are in themselves
aspects of the goals of social development. Thus, when assessing
educational needs, attention must be paid to the aspects of education (other than the skill-producing function of the school) that
facilitate broad social conditions favorable to economic growth
and to the other goals of social development. Unfortunately,
however, the outcomes of schooling other than skills have thus
far not been measured with precision.

[20]Adam Curle, *Educational Planning in Pakistan* (Cambridge: Harvard University Press, 1966), p. 42.

Finally, assessment of needs, which gives consideration only to education in quantitative terms, is exceedingly crude. Ultimately, educational planning must concern itself with questions regarding the quality of education. There are several definitions of quality, including those that pertain to the degree of sophistication and specialization of academic work, namely, whether a given educational task is performed efficiently, and the degree to which fundamental truths are found. For the sake of staying close to the practical problems of planning, let us consider a particular definition of quality that relates to the efficiency of the educational effort in getting given tasks done—for example, provision of necessary motivations, understandings, and level and number of skills.

In this sense, quality might be affected by such factors as the amount of time spent in school (schools in Western Europe and certain other parts of the world run several weeks longer per year than those in America), and advances in educational technology and greater scientific insight into learning characteristics. (A vicious circle is represented here, for better-educated communities tend to have higher-quality schools.) Yet evidence as to the effects of these factors on the amount of learning is difficult, if not impossible, to find. Thoroughly understanding the social consequences of such factors is our ultimate goal, but a target seemingly far distant at the present time. Yet the "qualitative" problem manifests itself very directly even in the manpower approach to planning, where specific skills are translated into numbers of years of schooling or lengths of particular vocational courses.

In an earlier chapter it was argued that the possible contributions of education to development are numerous and subtle. Education functions to produce changed behavior not only in the manpower sense but also in the wider political and social sense. By selecting, promoting, and certifying individuals on the basis of talent, education functions to create equality of opportunity. Further, as a distributor of knowledge and the tools for acquiring more knowledge, education may modify value patterns and systems of political action.

The question thus arises whether the functions of education, other than its role in relation to manpower, can be made sufficiently concrete to be translated into meaningful educational

policies.   At present, the answer would seem to be that research
is not yet able to suggest the structure and content of education
best suited to foster development.   This does not imply, however,
that the considered judgment of knowledgeable educators may
not be used as the basis for planning.   For example, a clear "philosophy of education" needs to be established, supported by both
political and educational leaders, and understood by at least a
significant portion of the population.   The use of education as an
instrument for social change requires identification of the values
to be transferred to current and subsequent generations.   Hopefully, educational research will increasingly be able to shed light
on the manner in which such values may be more efficiently
transmitted.

In order to measure with more precision the societal benefits to
be secured from an educational system, new and better educational and social measures are needed.   Some attempts have been
made to develop better measures of the output of educational
systems by utilizing more pertinent data than such typical measures as literacy, numbers of graduates, and enrollment ratios.[21]
Measures of the behavioral outputs of schooling, linked to social
and economic variables in careful historical studies (data being
available), might prove valuable in telling us more about the
contributions of various educational programs.   Another possibility would be small-scale experimental studies of how different
educational programs interact with the wider social context.   A
substantial amount of theory regarding behavior-change is available, but unfortunately it is rarely drawn upon to link schools
with other local institutions in a program of planned change.
Comparative studies of the record of various national systems
of education are a third possibility (although the fruitfulness of
these would depend, in turn, on refined methodology in the study
of education in the process of social change).

Some Operational Problems

The educational case studies of Middle Africa, South Asia, and
Latin America, presented earlier, illustrate several of the difficul-

---

[21] See, for example, the analyses of the "pupil hour" and the "pass year" educational measures found in Adams and Farrell, *op. cit.*

ties and pitfalls in the educational planning process. The problems of inadequate data, inefficient administrative machinery, conflicts between developmental goals and social demand, and conceptual misunderstandings may all be found in the planning efforts in developing nations.

In Latin America, for example, most nations have established structures to provide educational planning services, and much formal educational planning has been undertaken with apparent political support. Yet the results in terms of relating educational change to national goals have been disappointing. Educational plans frequently have been mere reports, and not the means for action. In effect, the forces that influence quantitative and qualitative changes in education have not been harnessed by the planning apparatus.

The reasons for the shortcomings in educational planning in Latin America are probably too numerous and subtle to elaborate here. Clearly, however, the basic difficulty is not one of financial resources. Blame could more accurately be placed on such factors as political instability, resistance within the educational system itself, and inefficiency in the administrative structure. Regarding the latter point, the coordination between ministries of education and central planning bodies is often lacking, as is liaison at the higher level between planning bodies and political authorities. Indeed, in some Latin American nations, the educational data collected by one government agency are rarely made available to other government agencies.

The problems encountered in educational planning in several African nations are of a different nature. The administrative structures necessary to carry out the planning process are generally less well developed than in Latin America. Moreover, the financial constraints on educational growth are extremely severe.

On the other hand, many of the new African nations appear intent on making educational decisions in a careful and rational manner. Most of the former British colonial areas have conducted studies of available educational resources and have made estimates of manpower needs. Tanzania, for example, has shown remarkable constraint in arresting the unplanned expansion of school enrollments. An attempt is being made to hold primary-school enrollment at its present level in order to allocate resources for the expansion of secondary and higher education. Thus, even in an "infant republic" the euphoria of independence that envisioned schooling for all, and the romantic aspirations of educators in the same direction can be blunted by the rationality of the planner.

India and Pakistan represent nations in which the structure for educational planning is reasonably well developed and where rather sophisticated exercises in planning are being carried out. Yet, in both nations, political and social pressures have drastically altered educational change from the direction identified in the national plans. The planners have consistently argued for approximately equivalent rates of expansion at the primary- and secondary-school levels; however, during each planning period, the proportionate increase in enrollments has been greater in secondary education. Such inability to control the growth of secondary (and postsecondary) education apparently reflects the lack of acceptance of the plan objectives by those in a position to influence plan implementation. In India, much of the burden of the implementation of educational planning must rest with the state governments, but state officials appear to take little action to check enrollments at any educational level.

Summary

Some developing nations appear to be succeeding without extensive centralized planning. Some nations with elaborate governmental mechanisms for planning are developing at a very slow rate. Mexico and Ceylon might be taken as examples of the former, while India and several Latin American nations might fit the latter category. Yet the issue is never "to plan or not to plan," but rather, the extent and rationality of planning and the degree to which it is centralized. Planning, at least in accordance with some crude standard and at some administrative level, is present in all nations.

Two important constraints on any approach to educational planning should be reemphasized. First, the analysis of educational needs without consideration of the cost involved remains merely academic; yet, a surprising amount of the activity that goes on under the name of educational planning gives little attention to the constraints of a national fiscal ability. In a sense, plans are often confused with planning; for the plan is but a document, while planning is a continuous process involving constant reassessment of social and economic benefits. Second, making decisions regarding alternative investments, such as education, public health, and defense, is at least partly a political act. This means not only that successful planning (although not necessarily a technically successful plan) will depend on the interest of political leaders but also that the political leaders give substance to educational targets. Priorities and organizational solutions must reflect political intentions:

> If the primary objective is improvement of the planning process rather than the preparation of a comprehensive plan, planners cannot start, as they frequently do, with a series of theoretical abstractions of planning as it ought to be and try to force them on an inhospitable environment where governments are unstable, not genuinely committed to development or otherwise unready for advanced planning. Instead...they must attempt to mold their ... plans to "things as they are."... Emphasis [should] be given to micro-economic aspects of planning, to sound policy formation and improved organization.[22]

In the absence of ability to predict the necessary mix of skills, knowledge, and motivation needed at each subsequent phase of the development process (or even to what degree development is related to particular characteristics of human resources), educational planning frequently degenerates into projections of educational expansion. Such projections are based on the rate of growth and expected composition of population age, the current enrollment, the dropout rates, and the contemporary educational structure. This form of planning may be of considerable value administratively and may be an important step toward more comprehensive and integrated national educational planning. Yet this approach cannot be more than an interim measure, for it rejects a basic purpose of planning—namely, the organization and utilization of human beings and their values in order to create

---

[22] Waterston, *op. cit.*, p. 9–10.

new institutions and human relationships vastly different from those currently in existence. Uncertainty regarding our capabilities in achieving this goal should not mean the rejection of planning in favor of mere projections, but rather, more, albeit cautious, attention to planning.

Suggested Readings for Chapter VII

ADAMS, DON, ed. *Educational Planning*. Syracuse: Syracuse University Press, Center for Development Education, 1964.

ANDERSON, C. ARNOLD. "Educational Planning in the Context of National Social Policy," *Phi Delta Kappan*, Vol. 47, No. 4 (December 1965).

BEREDAY, GEORGE, *et al.*, eds. *The World Yearbook of Education, Educational Planning*. New York: Harcourt, Brace & World, 1967.

CORREA, HECTOR. *Educational Planning: Its Quantitative Aspects and Its Integration with Economic Planning*. Paris: International Institute for Educational Planning, 1963.

CURLE, ADAM. "Some Aspects of Educational Planning in Underdeveloped Areas," *Harvard Educational Review*, Vol. 32, No. 3 (Summer 1962).

DAVIS, RUSSELL. *Planning Human Resource Development*. Chicago: Rand McNally, 1966.

Economic and Social Aspects of Educational Planning. Paris: UNESCO, 1964.

The Forecasting of Manpower Requirements. Washington: Department of State, AID, 1963.

LYONS, RAYMOND, ed. *Problems and Strategies of Educational Planning*. Paris: UNESCO, IIEP, 1965. See especially Chapter III, pp. 45–63.

PLATT, WILLIAM J. *Conflict in Educational Planning*. Menlo Park, Calif.: Stanford Research Institute, 1962.

SANDERS, DONALD P. *Some Qualitative Aspects of Education in Educational Planning*. Paris: OECD, 1963.

Social Objectives in Educational Planning. Paris: OECD, 1967.

WATERSTON, ALBERT. *Development Planning*. Baltimore: Johns Hopkins Press, 1965.

INDEX

Adamson, J. W., 26–27
African tribal groups, 58–60
Armytage, W. H. G., 24–25

Balogh, T., 127
Baron, Paul A., 45
Becker, Howard S., 124–125
Bowen, William G., 43
Brave, Vinoba, 82
Brembeck, Cole S., 95
British External Examinations, 50
Buddhism, 76
Bulsara, Jal F., 85–86

Cash, Webster C., 151
Curle, Adam, 152
Curriculum and development, 24–26,
  32–33, 35, 68, 69, 72–73, 77–78, 83,
  91, 93, 101–102, 113, 114, 117,
  127–129, 136

Detribalization, 54–55, 57
Development, contemporary characteristics, 4–6
  educational, 9–10
  historical English views, 2–4
  modern theories, 7–8
  social differentiation, 10–12
  vicious and beneficent circle theories,
  12–15
Development and language diversity,
  55–56, 79
Development and population change,
  22–23, 38–42, 86–87, 103
Development and religious and value
  systems, 58–60, 80–83, 103–105,
  134–137
Development and urbanization, 56–58,
  83–86
Dropouts, 68, 91, 110, 115–116, 125–
  127

Education and communications, 21
Education and demography, 22–23,
  38–42, 86–88, 107–108, 133

Education and development, in devel-
  oped countries, 21–23
  in developing countries, 23–36, 36–45
Education and the economy, 42–43
Education and language, 55–56, 79
Education and the law, 21
Education and manpower, 41, 66, 70–
  71, 91, 116, 145–148, 150–151
Education and national goals, 60–73,
  152
Education and the polity, 43–45, 60–64
Education and production and trade,
  21
Education and rural development,
  109–110
Education and social class, 65, 78–79,
  84, 95–97, 101–102, 114, 117
Education and social mobility, 59, 65–
  67, 85, 88
Education and technology, 22
Education and unemployment, 57–58,
  69
Education and urbanization, 57–58,
  84–86, 111–112, 129–131
Educational demand, 38, 58–60, 111,
  112, 113, 114, 126–127, 148–149
Educational development, 9–10
Educational enrollment, 20, 33, 57–58,
  62, 64, 66, 68, 69, 70, 71, 78, 84–85,
  86, 88, 93, 94, 105, 106, 108, 110,
  130–131
Educational expenditure, 42–43, 50, 91,
  105–106, 108
Educational opportunity, 51, 55, 57–58,
  61–67, 68, 78, 83, 84–85, 95–97,
  101–102, 109, 110, 130, 149
Educational planning, 41, 52, 67–71,
  88–94, 105–106, 140–158
  criticism of, 148–151
  definition of, 141–143
  goals of, 143–148
  operational problems, 154–156
Elites, 7, 8, 26, 37, 51, 64, 65, 78–79, 83,
  94–97, 101

England, dissenter academies, 24–25
    Factory Acts, 28–30
    Royal Society, 25–26

Female education, 33–34, 68, 85, 88,
    131–133
Foster, George M., 38, 67

Gandhi, Mahatma, 93
Government of India Act (1919), 78

Harbison, Frederick H., and Charles
    A. Myers, 9–10, 126
Herskovits, Melville J., 53
Higher education, 9, 134
    in England, 25, 30–31
    in Japan, 32–33
    in Latin America, 102, 105, 110,
        116–120
    in Middle Africa, 53, 67, 69–71
    in South Asia, 78, 79, 85, 87, 88, 91,
        95, 96, 133–134
Hinduism, 76, 80–81
Hooke, Robert, 25–26

Isbister, John, 40–41
Islam, 76, 78, 80

Japan, compulsory education, 34, 36
    Education Law (1872), 34–35
    Imperial Rescript on Education
        (1890), 35
    Institute for the Study of Barbarian
        Writings, 32
    introduction of Western learning, 32
    Meiji period, 34–36
    Shingaku, 33
    Terakoya, 34
    Tokugawa period, 32–34

Kabir, Humayin, 44
Karachi Plan, 92
Kuznets, Simon, 39

Latin, America, colonial educational
        policies, 100–102
    Catholic church and education,
        100–102
    cultural variations and education,
        102–103

Leach, A. F., 27
Leibenstein, Harvey, 14–15
Literacy, 20, 21, 26–28, 33–34, 36, 38,
    53, 76, 84, 85, 86, 109, 131
Lombard, Frank, 32–33

Malthus, Thomas Robert, 3–4
Marx, Karl, 7–8
Middle Africa, Belgian educational
        policies, 52–53
    British educational policies, 49–50
    cultural variations in receptivity to
        change, 58–60
    French educational policies, 49–52
    languages, 55–56
    missionary education, 49, 53, 55
Migration, 56, 57, 58, 85, 86, 103,
    109–110, 129
Montagu, Ashley, 131–132
Myers, Charles Nash, 110
Myint, H., 16–17
Myrdal, Gunnar, 13–14

Nash, Manning, 109
Nationalism, 60, 83
Northrup, F. S. C., 81
Nurske, Ragnar, 13
Nyerere, Julius K., 72–73

Ottenberg, Simon and Phoebe, 53–54

Parsis, 82
Parsons, Talcott, 10–12
Passin, Herbert, 33
Pipkin, Charles W., 30
Primary education, 124, 125, 132, 145
    in England, 29
    in Japan, 34–36
    in Latin America, 108, 110–113
    in Middle Africa, 49, 50, 51, 53, 57,
        62, 66, 68, 73
    in South Asia, 79, 84, 86, 87, 90–92,
        93, 96
Purdah, 80

Regional planning, 69–70, 91, 145
Ricardo, David, 3
Rostow, Walt W., 7–8

Saint-Simon, 4
Sargent, W. L., 27

Schwartz, Harry, 133–134
Secondary education, 9, 124, 134
    in England, 24–25
    in Latin America, 105, 108, 110,
        113–116
    in Middle Africa, 49, 57, 64, 66, 67,
        68, 69, 70, 71, 73
    in South Asia, 78, 79, 85, 87, 90–91,
        95, 96
Shaw, George Bernard, 31
Singer, Milton, 82
Sismondi, 4
Smelser, Neil J., 10–12, 23–24, 28–29,
    37
Smith, Adam, 2–3
South Asia, basic education, 93–94

effects of colonial rule, 76–79
    Moslem education, 78, 132
    religious and value system, 80–83
Stycos, J. Mayone, 41–42

Teacher education, 35, 69, 125
Teacher shortage, 71, 92, 93, 108, 117,
    124–125
Thrupp, S. L., 26

Vocational education, 52, 53, 78, 90,
    91, 105, 127–128, 146–147

Wagley, Charles, and Marvin Harris,
    102–103